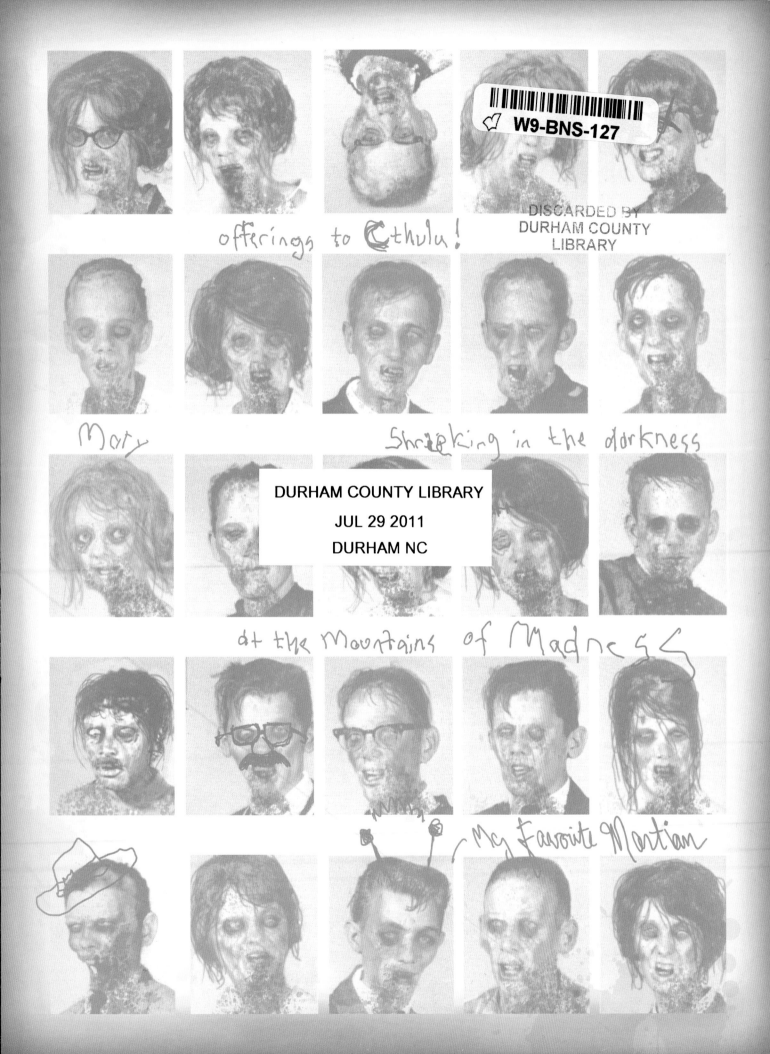

offerings to Cthulu!

Mary

Shrieking in the darkness

at the Mountains of Madness

My Favorite Martian

ZOMBIE HIGH

yearbook '64

created by Jeff Busch

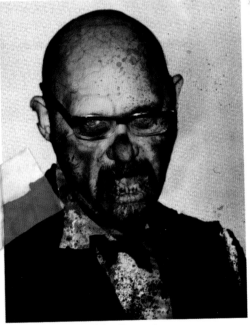

Mr. Busch
Graduating Class Counselor

STERLING
New York

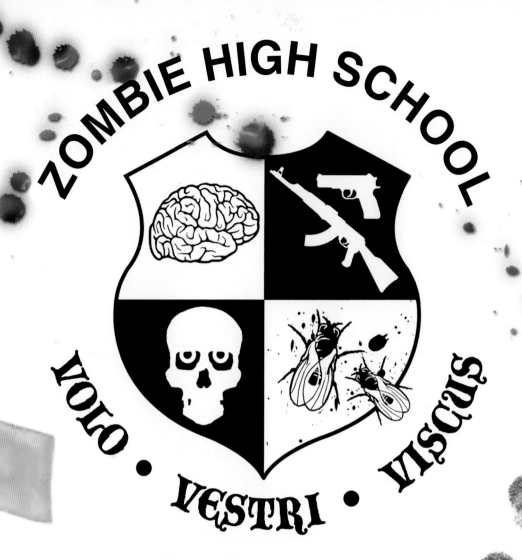

ZOMBIE HIGH SCHOOL

VOLO • VESTRI • VISCUS

Revenant's Cry

'Neath the sloughing of the fetid flesh,
'Neath wet and rancid organs black,
Our brains sense meat, our nose-holes blood,
We shall come crawling back

(repeat, gnash, claw)

From shallow graves in dampened earth
From basements damp and cold
We shamble out and through and up
to wail this song of old

(repeat, gnash, claw)

We howl for thee, Grand Zombie High
Mouthless screams of hungered pain
We gnaw and bite here in the dark
And hope our stalking be not in vain.

(long, wailing scream)

Contents

Abandon hope, all ye who enter here!

Greeting, Salutations and Honors ....Pages 4-9

Grounds and Facilities ....Pages 10-13

Faculty ....Pages 14-21

Support Staff ....Pages 22-26

Athletics ....Pages 27-37

Exchange Student and Student Personalities ....Pages 38-46

Academic Achievements ....Pages 47-49

Social Events ....Pages 50-58

Clubs and Organizations ....Pages 59-73

Student Gallery ....Pages 74-76

Graduating Seniors ....Pages 77-94

Junior Class ....Pages 95-105

Sophomore Class ....Pages 106-113

Freshmen Class ....Pages 114-121

In Memoriam ....Pages 122-124

Our Sponsors ....Pages 125-128

Beware the detention trough!

Cafe Roland?

Ha!

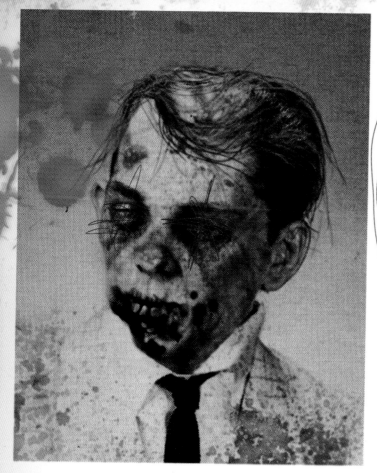

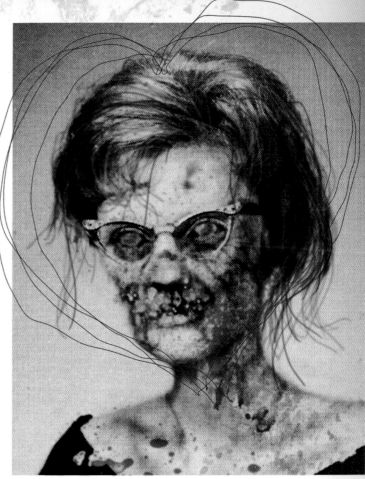

Skip Drordy
Co-Editor

Becky Hanson
Co-Editor

The 1963/1964 school year has been one of tremendous change and growth for us all, individually and as a nation. The inspiring speech by Dr. King on the Mall followed a mere three months later by tragic loss of President Kennedy has made for a year of extremes. Though some might say these events divide us, I think they knit us more closely and make us stronger. Let's all hope that the rest of the '60s will offer a safe, quiet stretch of sanity, security, and peace. And brains.

Politics and war are certainly cause for concern in these topsy-turvy times, but ladies fashions and cosmetics for 1964 and beyond look to be a dream come true. With advances in skin replacement products, stylish new boots and shoes, and a little something called the mini-skirt, young women of today are certain to be asked for more than just a fresh cup of coffee. Plus, the Beatles are here, and do they ever look scrumptious!

Howard F. Koger
Superintendent District 7

Dear Graduates,

What you have learned during your years here at Zombie High will serve your future ventures in good stead. Whether you are intent on serving your great Nation overseas, engineering the first rocketship to take an American (Living or otherwise) to the moon, or aimlessly shuffling about the countryside in search of quivering human tissue, the tools you have gained here will be of immeasurable aid. The habits impressed upon you by your teachers of punctuality, of scholarship, and of quickly stapling shut any wounds you receive as you wrestle your meals into submission will only grow in value. You are entering a world of changes and challenges and I will expect you to leave your mark on it. I have no doubt that, as graduates of this fine institution, you have been faithfully and meaningfully prepared to grab the world by the neck and sink your remaining stable teeth into its brainpan.

Irwin DeBold
Principal

My fellow Undead,

It is with great honor that I now call you Revenants, Graduates of Zombie High Class of 1964. In the days, weeks, and possibly years ahead you may recall through a foggy haze your time spent here. Wherever you venture, wherever the afterlife may take you, always try to remember that you were a part of Zombie High.

Si vos reprehendo is edo caput capitis primoris!

Dr. Charles Neidart
A Message From The Coroner

Greetings, Infected, and congratulations on completing your high school education.

It is my legal duty to inform you that as you begin to roam the streets of our city without any institutional supervision, there is a distinct possibility that you will be decapitated, shot in the head, or incinerated with a flamethrower (likely the county sheriff department's newly issued, Australian-made M2A1-7 portable models).

Good luck with your future endeavors for survival.

Grounds & Facilities

East Entrance
– Lunch Break?

Save some for me.

Newly-Remodeled Main Entrance
– School's Out!

Sadie Hawkins Dance
Saturday, April 11

Who's the new guy?

Entrance to Original School
– Good Memories

Recently Remodeled Gymnasium – Go Revenants!

Our Hallowed Halls – Caution! Wet Floor!

Detention Trough – Uh-Oh, someone forgot to stay on school grounds!

Grounds & Facilities

Romero Auditorium
New Velvet & Paint over the Holidays has really brightened up the place

DO NOT ENTER
have a nice day!

The Hammer Studio aka Campus Cremation Compound
Have a Nice Day!

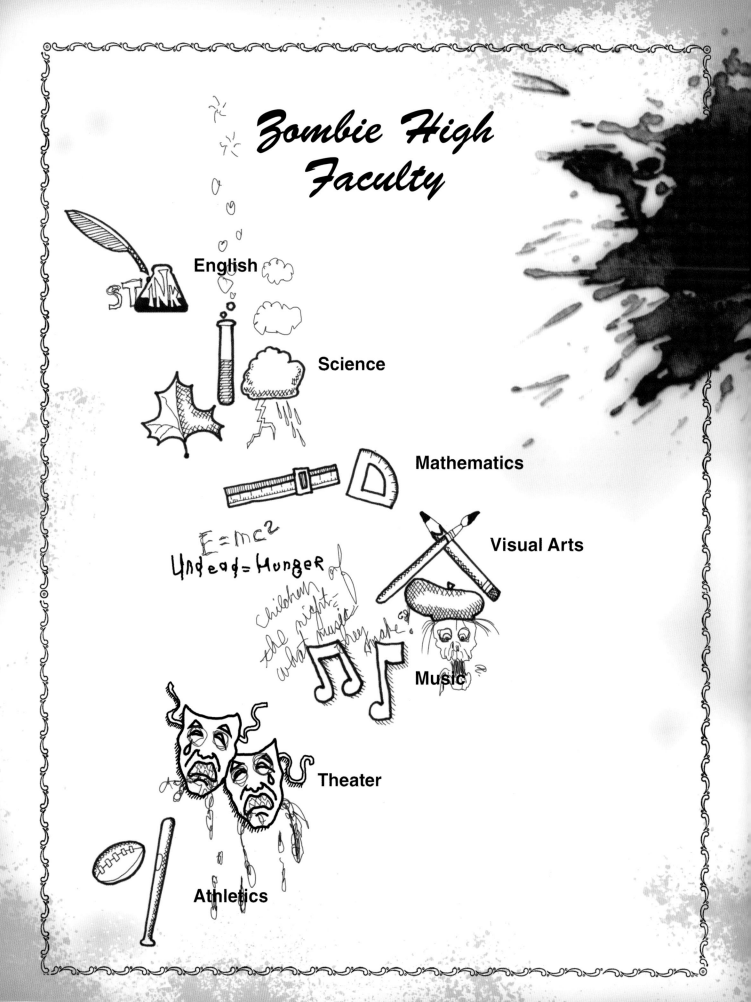

Zombie High Faculty

English

Science

Mathematics

$E = mc^2$

Undead = Hunger

Visual Arts

Music

Theater

Athletics

Faculty
English & Literature

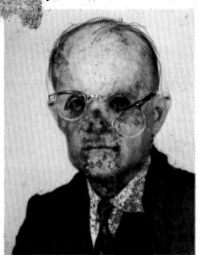

Dr. Leonard Wright

 *She's "HOT" for you*

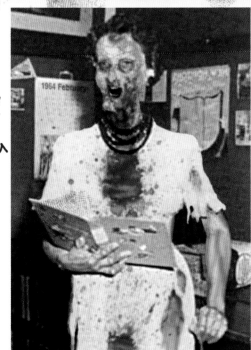

Mrs. Prudence Hume
(cremated)

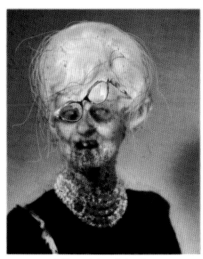

Miss Hochholter

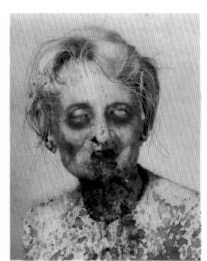

Miss Marion Dipboye

 *Best Wishes, M. Ulmer*

Mr. Edward Ulmer

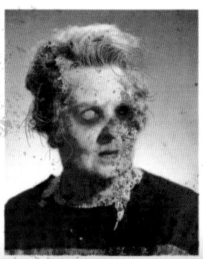

Miss Jean Parisi

...ear's to you!

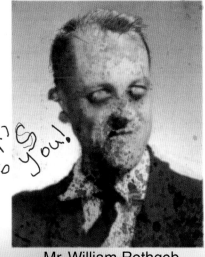

Mr. William Rothgeb

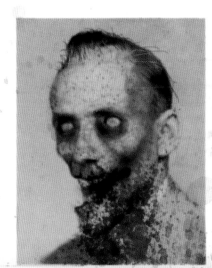

Mr. Verlin Hallam

Dr. Evert Wray (retired)

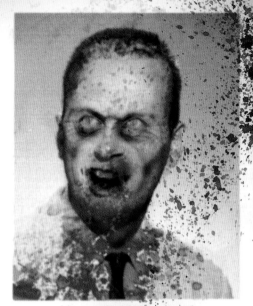

Kenneth Wildermuth

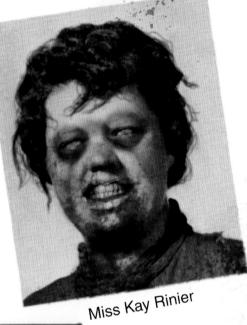

Miss Kay Rinier

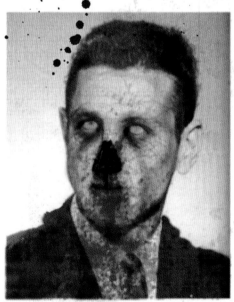

Dave Tuberty

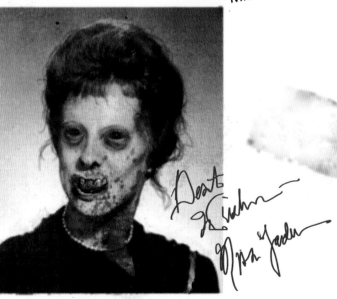

Miss Doris Yader

Faculty
Mathematics

Harold Wolfe

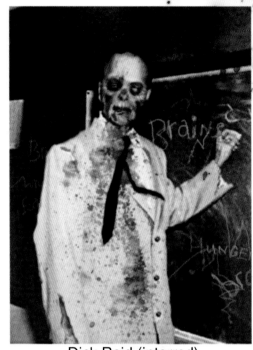

Dick Reid (interred)

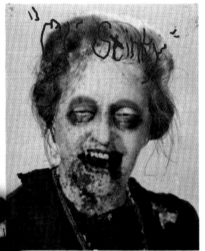

Mrs. Bonnie Eagan

Michael Muzzillo

Harold Bixler

Parasites are making it hard to write.

James Gerni

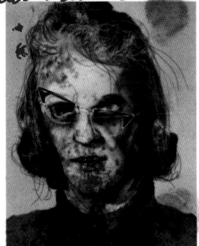

Miss Fran Lehnus

Faculty
Visual Arts

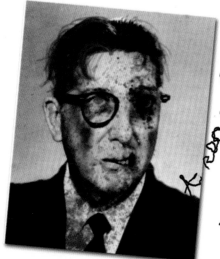

Dr. Roger Douwes

Did she trace that?

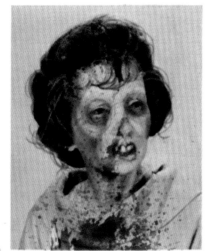

Miss Jane Parente

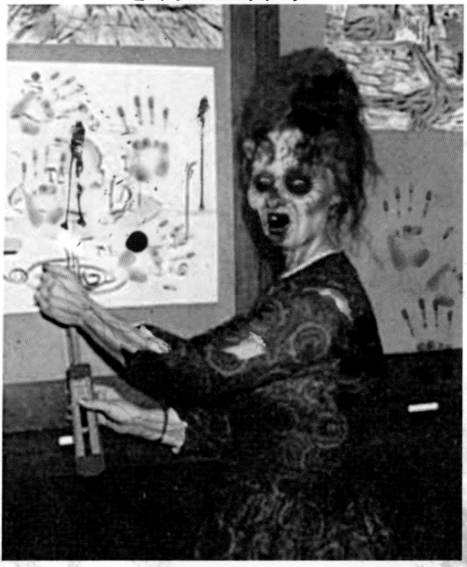

Mrs. Sandra Luxem

Miss Mary Ellen Linton
(dismembered & cremated)

Faculty
Visual Arts

...ssel Pfaff

Ella Rudig

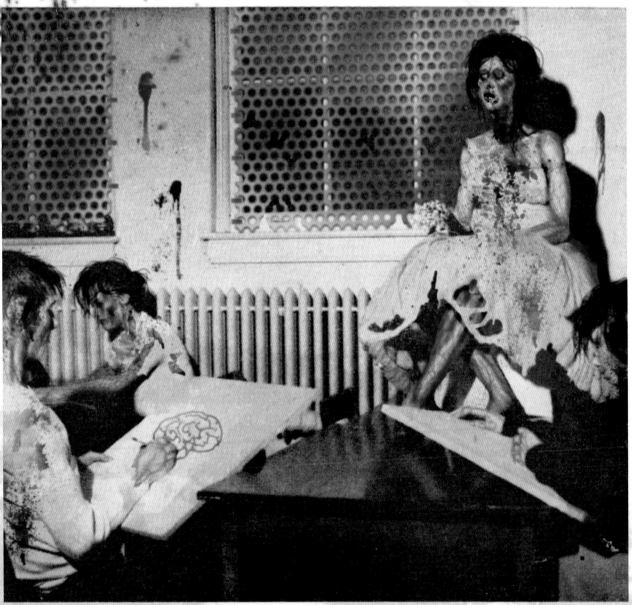

The lovely Miss Vonnett Belcher poses for fellow students in Mr. Pfaff's Drawing 101 Class

Faculty

To my very favorite student!
Best Wishes,
Mr. Blume

Mr. Roger Fultz; Miss Edith Bauer; Mr. Dennis Blume;
Mrs. Nan Barger harmonize at the Music Room podium

Music

Miss Dorcas VanDeMear
(decapitated)

Faculty
Theater & Performing Arts

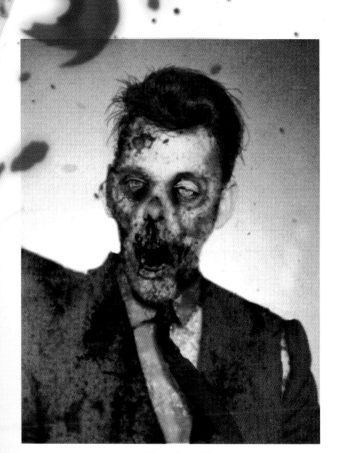

Mr. Charles Zier

Making Sweet Music Together!!

Mr. David McCain and Miss Katheryn O'Reilly
perform at the March Talent Show

This place is for "The Birds"!
← BIRD

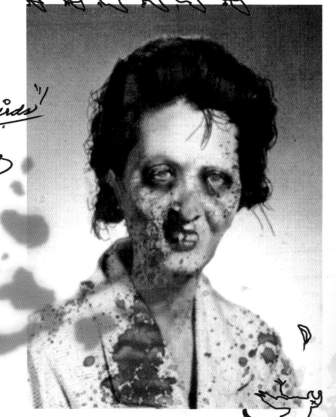

Mrs. Edna Sherman

Support Staff
Building Maintenance

The Three Musketeers! Davey Wysong; Stan Bowles; Pat Moon

The ever-vigilant Ronnie Myers cleaning the
ever-slippery floors of East Wing

Support Staff
Cafeteria ~~mmm~~ mm-Good

Mrs. Mary Newman oversees her staff of Mrs. Shirley Ott;
Miss Sandra Minks; Miss Bonnie Bulick; Mrs. Arlene Boughton

Thursday Surprise!

Grey Matter & Sweetbreads Stew

Support Staff
Disposal Detail

Mr. Black is always suited and prepared to aid in any disposal or containment emergency that might arise. Can't sneak up on him!

Support Staff
Grounds

Head Groundskeeper Paulie Scheerer extricates a new student unfamiliar with the school's landscaping.

Assistant Groundskeeper Stash Czelinski proves that having a "green thumb" (even when it used to belong to someone else) can be a real advantage when tending to the roses near the South Pits.

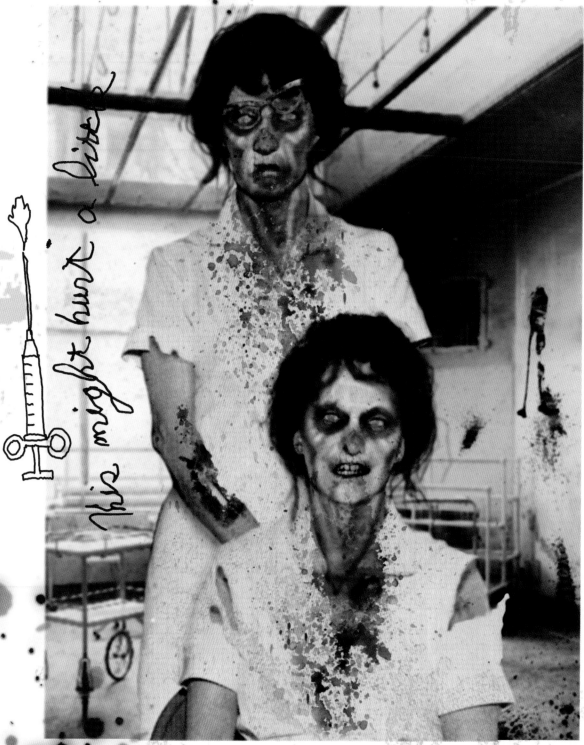

This might hurt a little

RN Janalyce Sheperd and her new assistant LPN Beverly Wasson
were always ready to dispense bandages, cauterize or
reattach lost limbs, and administer staples as needed.
Thanks for keeping us together!

Athletics

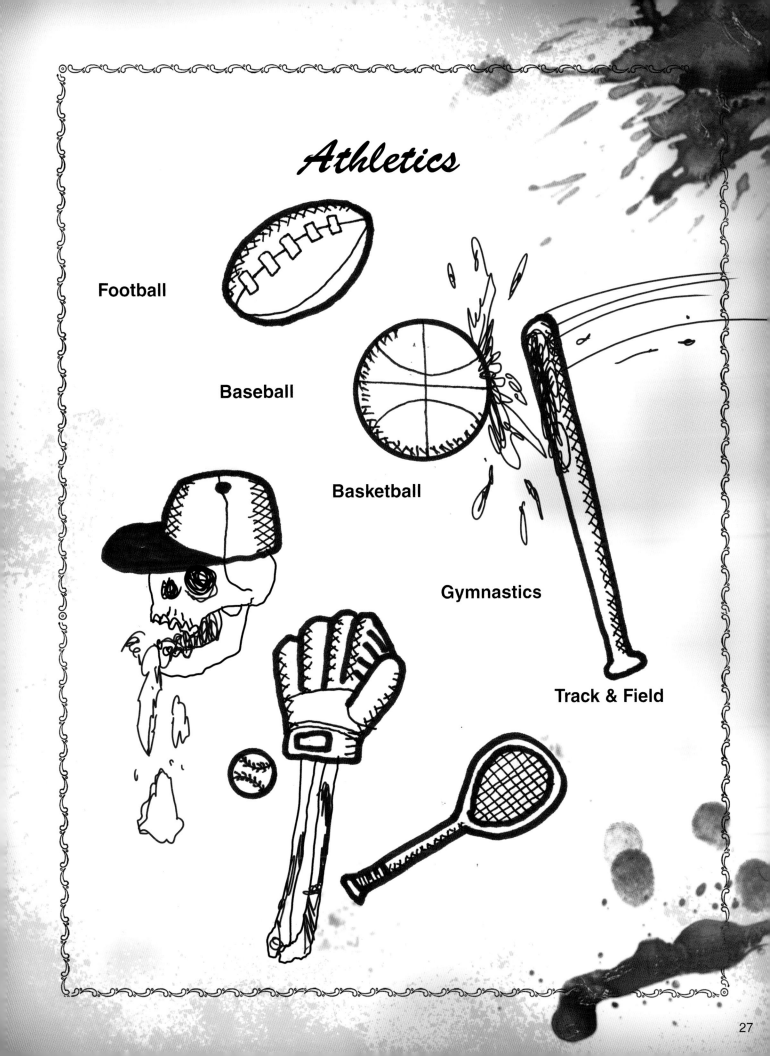

Football

Baseball

Basketball

Gymnastics

Track & Field

Athletics
Football: Senior Squad

Assistant Coach F. D. Jackson; Team Doctor Robert McMahon; Assistant Coach Dale Beck; Al Curl; Kirby Yoder; Jim "Toxic" Netolicky; Larry Scullion; John Zellers; Gary Rohrer; Mike Glaser; Don Culp; Donald Garwood; Eric Snyder; Jim Keck; George "Grey Matter" Wickline; F. K. Donalds; Lee Veon; Paul Douglas; Jim Weaver; Erle Meade; Mike Simpson; Charles Hockinson; David Hum; Thomas Wentzler; Arlen Flynn; Pat Smith; Charles "Chuck" Russell; Larry Theiss; Willard Scott; Fred Oeler; Jim Cleveland; Olaf "Offal" Swedson; Edward Steckla; Jerry Browning; Lyle Lohan; Assistant Coach Shasteen; Equipment Manager Roloff

Team Captain John Zellers is about to give his opponent the ol' what-fer!

Co-Captain Flynn is ready to pounce!

Coach Dromph; Tom Apinis; Chris Barrow; Mike Altomare; Phillip Oliver; Jim Grant; Patrick Dunbar; Mitch "The Itch" Gayon; David "Rest In" Peece; Larry VanFossen; Barry Jones; Bart Puscher; Herb Drotleff; Tom "Roller" Over; Bill Hawkins; Rodney Reil; Jim Havey; Bob Miller; Rex Ambrose; Martin Cosentino, Equipment Manager Teddy Kacenski; Coach Crnkovitch

The team plows through the competition without even considering a quick snack.

The Revenants take cross-county rivals, the Springfield Eagles, to pieces in the state finals in a thrilling 21-20 nailbiter.

Robert Wilms; Geoffrey Leonard; Ron "Greenie" Parsley; John Rhoades; Pat Cunningham; Jason Labeau; Tom Downes; Joe Fitzpatrick; Stephen "Eatin'" Eaton; Kurt Schmidt; William Orr; Reggie Shingleton; Craig Eisenhower; David French; Stan Berryman; Lee Stamets; Randy "Dead Leg" Morrison; Tyler Reash; Mark Basinger; Jack Carr; Roger Cook; Rick Finley; Allen Mamis; Greg Madden; Keith Gormely; Art Hall; Joe Vinaklins; Rick Blackburn; Dick Burklo; Don Shirilla; Robin Keyser; Laurence Newcomer; Matthew Holderread; Dennis Shodd; Steven Forney; Curtis Van Dyke; Albert Bowman; James Eisenwein; Saul Wining; Irv "The Gruesome" LeGrou; Albert Portnoy; Robert Champney; Danny Young; Ricky "Rickets" Kendall; John Dennis; Patrick Kuhlman; Alfred McKee; Paul Magill; Michael "Rotting" Rodman; Kenny Echard; Equipment Manager Larry Munyon; Coach Rinehart

Assistant Coaches Lou Sportseller; Fred Cyrus (cremated); Eddie Pictros; Mark Stacey (cremated)

Ooops!

Coach Henry Dromph; Bruce Dowd; Duane Crowl; Glenn Schmidt; Mark Weyman; Terrance "The Lip" Lippman; John Roher; David Garver; Jeff Griffith; Don Blakeman; Eugene "Entrails" Wise; Donal O'Hara; Danny Peters; Ken Hughes; Bill Johnson; Robin Bussard; Lee Hamilton; Tom Wilkoff; Doug Ziegler; not pictured: Rex Wetzel (interred)

Jim Keck gets ready to hit another dinger out of the park!

RIP Coach Dunphey. You will be missed.

Hammerin' Hank?

Dennis Taylor; Jim Ward; Donald McBane; Thomas Kiebler; Sandy Robbins; Marvin Yeager;
David Savage; Alan Wyndsock; James Harding; Ronnie Witmer; Jeff Brode;Rod Pietrus; Max Thiedt;
Tommy Morrison; Danny Lehman; Todd La Londe; not pictured: Timothy Court, Equipment Manager

Marvin Yeager 'rounds third base
on his way to home plate!

Tommy Wardrip; Jack Gaughan; Homer Gregg; Dean Color; Thomas Suffolk; Dale Smith; David Houlette; Keith Sposetta; Ted Westfall; Daniel Lipe; Jack Troyer; Equipment Manager Verne McGrath; Interim Coach E.W. Book

Coach Weber

Jack Gaughan going for that jumpshot!

nt Coach Theadore Dressler; Tate Snyder; Rick Lawrence; Colin Hawkins; Dick Troll;
ke; Alan "Stretch" Barnes; Kirby Perrin; Phil Ward; Jim Gosney; Phil Burbick; William "Bill"
rick; Joey Young; Equipment Manager Thom Chesney; Rob Tharp; Paul Kisner; Bill Hartman;
Bonkowlski

An opposing player does their best to avoid coming in contact with our star forward!

Rich Lake is quite proficient with ball-handling.

Stan Ferrall; Dick Wilms; Dale Foertch; Wilder Bailey; Ray Gloss; Eldon Keylor; George Weems; Robert "Bob" Gessler; Waldo Merrill; Coach Fultz

Where's the mat?

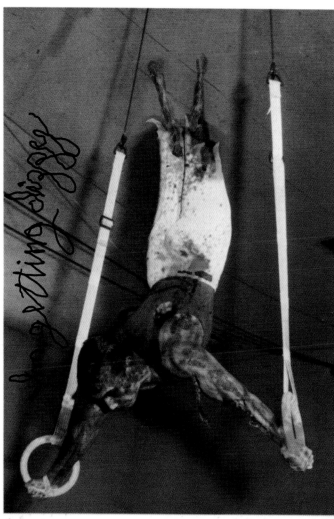

This isn't so tough, but nailing the landing is hard with no feet!

Athletics
Girls Sports

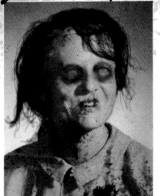

Miss M. Maurer
Girls Coach

Miss America Pageant

ooh la-la!

Our lovely Field Hockey Team.
What a becoming group of talented young ladies!

Not bad for girls—

Watch those sticks!

Morning calisthenics with
Miss Pogartz

E-Z

EASY

E-Z

P.G.
uh-oh
E-Z
Our young ladies after a tough match — not much time to fix that hair, girls!

Thomas Wick; Carl Andermann; Dave Prohaskas; Steve Wright; Ken Lysne; Scott Holmstrom; Richard Helmsely; Mitch Ogden; Tom Bookwalter; Brian Gantz; Robert Berryman; Coach Bonkowlski

Be sure to let go of that baton, Steve!

Don't take my arm!!

Coach Winston

Uh-oh, there goes another tibia & fibula…

37

Exchange Student
Bon Appetit!

City of Lights Mon Dieu!

Oui Oui You! You!

French Kiss

alimentation
française est
delicious

This year we welcomed the lovely Miss Marie Cocteau, our exchange student from Calais, France. Miss Cocteau entertained us with her lilting recitals of Edith Piaf songs and some fascinating discussions regarding the differences between the wine-growing regions of Bordeaux, including the Médoc, Graves, Pomerol, and St. Émilion.

No dilettante regarding the culinary arts either, Marie exhibited an encyclopedic knowledge of the preparation & presentation of all the organ meats, especially the thymus and pancreas.

Bon au revoir et etre bien!

Student Personalities

Most Dependable

Scott Davies and Mindy Barnes can always be counted on when in need of a helping hand (or other appendage)!

Say "Cheese"

I caught a fish this big!

Most Energetic

Ken Inglis and Jill Handy can't seem to sit still!

Student Personalities

"I "C" cup" hardly!

Most Refined

Peter Kalinowski and Georgette Murphy bring European class to any situation

Ho Ho How Painful

Santa?

Most Domestic

Becky Franko and James Mulvey whip up a special treat during the Holidays!

Student Personalities

Most Polite

Jean Maurer and William Simundza are always there to open a door, pull out a chair, or reattach a limb for you.

Cutest Couple Without Mandibles

Steve Galt and Theresa Oban still manage to get their sentiments across! We loved seeing them spoon.

Student Personalities

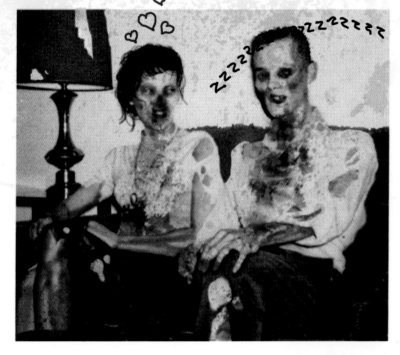

Most Romantic

Susan Wright and Carl Reigel spend some quiet time together before class—don't forget to eat, guys!

Most Promising Entrepreneurs

Chip Hutter and Francis Gregor show us "How to Succeed in Business Without Really Trying"!

Student Personalities

Most Flirtatious

Donald Brower and Kristen Minz never had trouble making new friends!

Oddest Couple

Sherry Jessen and Breather(!) Scott Bretcher made for an interesting pairing. RIP, Scott.

Student Personalities

Why won't he hold my hand?

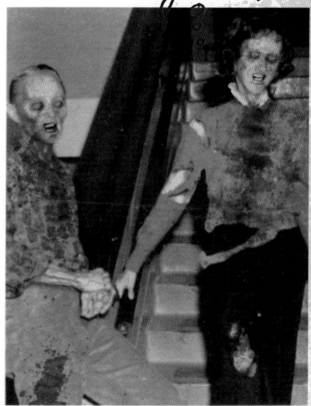

Mine!   *No, mine!*

Most Punctual
Davie Lindstrom and Yvonne Beiber never missed a bell!

Most Athletic
Geoff Burnham and Gloria Wilke were quite the couple on the hard-wood!

44

Student Personalities

Most Musical

Lawrence Mickle giving Candace Hanson some advice about her reed.

Best Dressed

Sharon Hall and Kenneth Tichy looking grand in their sweater vests—anything to keep the viscera in when the integuments begin to go!

Student Personalities

Best Read

See Dick Rot
Rot, Dick, Rot

Rot, Rot, Rot
Dick, Rot, Dick

Vincent Wilmouth and Jean Miller discuss the finer details of Lovecraft and the Necronomicon. As Abdul Alhazred tells us, "That is not dead which can eternal lie. And with strange aeons even death may die." Too true!

More tea, M'Lady?

You're Simply Charming!

Most Theatrical

Penny Osowski and Scott "Scotty" Adolphson enjoy an afternoon beverage.

Academic Achievements
Mathletes

$$A = \frac{\text{...}}{\sin(x+\theta)}$$

🦷 + 🦷 = 4

Pat Ard; Allen Beyer; Wain Dorway; Dick "Digits" Smith; David Ott; Michael Owens; John Bryan; Gregory Neary; Elizabeth Taggart

🧠 = Yummy

John Wolfe, Captain
Samantha Barile, Co-Captain

Academic Achievements
Decathlon

Squaresville

BruceWeiss; Patrice Remedi; Willy Eggert

Einstein Jr.

Marie Curie Jr.

Mary-Kate Fischer, Captain
Charles Dizak, Co-Captain

Academic Achievements
Intelli-Gents

Donald Fleming; Henry Stelter; James Anderson; Roger "Gassy" Passy

Is plaid their uniform?

Colleen Emery; Deirdre Grant; Sarah Barnes; Michelle Tillet; Karen Kennedy

Henry Erickson; Anna Heintz; Carole Danly; Craig Mason

Oppenheimer Jr.

Margaret Sangen Jr.

tramp

tramp

The Queen and her Court

BRAINS!

Varsity Football's Mouth-Watering Float

50

Dick+Liz

Dreamboat!

Hot-cha-cha!

Seriously, stop doing this crap

Homecoming King and Queen

King Charles "Chas" Killgore and his lovely Queen Beatrice Feldott
Who's the brains on this throne!

Social Events
Enchantment
Under The Earth

Thank You, Arthur Murray

Festive Decorations Abound!

A Night To Remember

Left foot,
right foot,
left foot
ha ha ha

I Want To Hold Your Hand

Food and Beverage Committee Prepares for a Magical Evening!

Mrs. Ed Gein

The Girls Finalizing The
Dance Banner

Social Events
Sadie Hawkins Dance

Looking Good, Scary Grant!

Looking Good!

David Farino Presents His Date with a Lovely Bouquet

Charlie Starkweather
Caril Fugate

lovely night for a bonfire – but don't get too close!

Who has the marshmallows?

OOPS! too close

Students dance by bonfire in celebration of the future.

Social Events
Samhain Festival

Bobbing for apples & other things

Our Evening's Mascot, "Guiser"

Our Festival King & Queen!

Promgoers arriving for the evening

Prom Queen Runners-Up
Mathilda Cleary and Wendy Freeman

Social Events
Prom 1964

Suture Self!

Our 1964 Prom Queen Sheryle Flynn

Prom King Charles Lestak, sadly, was immolated on his way to the dance. We'll miss you, Charlie!

Clubs & Organizations
Glee Club

Planning next year's shows?

Look Busy!!!

can·can·can NOT

Oooh-la-la!

DOE-RAY-MEAT·FA·SO·LA·TEETH·DOE!

Gather 'round the old Steinway for an impromptu sing-along.

Clubs & Organizations
Pep Squad

Blonde

Deadhead!

Claire Wright
Captain

Bonnie Hutter
Co-Captain

Debbie Collins

Brunette

Redhead

Hit'em
High
Hit'em
Low
Crack their
Skulls and
hungrily eat their
Brains!

Mary Meinke

Claire Simundza

Karen Oban

"2-4-6-8, when can we decapitate?
Go-o-o-o-o-o-o-o-o REVENANTS!"

Clubs & Organizations

Rembrandt's Studio

Suze Meyers and Stephanie Frey put the finishing touches on their silkscreen projects.

Nice Jackson Pollack!

Can't stay inside the lines ♡

Tim Stiben; Carl Melin; Roger Wycoff; Gary Larson; Mike Lipinski; Jeff Boone; Dean Fields; Bethany Ott; Jean Zimmerman; Louise Paddison; Mary Ann Morrow; Sarah Wahlgren

Clubs & Organizations
Languages Club

Our Students study world languages from Arabic to Zulu to Cthulu!

Eugene Stickels prepares
for his Spanish test

John Tusov presents his report on Central
Mexico – en Español! Mejor!

Your delicious, skill beating react you know he's right—

Tad Whitney; Esther Schaefer; Eleanor Thomas and Joanne Webster promote their political beliefs

Sadly, Chip was shot by a Jr. ROTC member at a Barry Goldwater rally. Sometimes, politics and dinner just don't mix.

Chip Anderson
Former Chairman

Clubs & Organizations
Quill & Scroll

Doing some "Railsplitting"!

ZZZZZZZZ

Edward Little; Nancy Banks; Mildred Castle; Bernice Schrey; Dot Weyland

Discussing an important plot point?

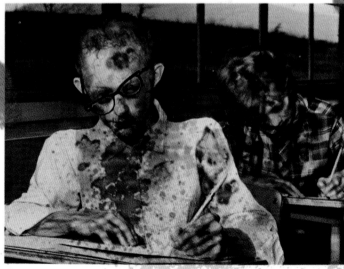

Mark Soreson is researching a new short story

The Morphy or Berlin Defense?

John Bobeck; Lester Maurer; David Gregor; Scott Wade; Leonard "Left Hemisphere" Lofgren; Wayne Foster; Harrison Dore; John Nechoda; Kenneth Puck; Jim Prince

Is it a Longines?

Yes! No. Yes! No.

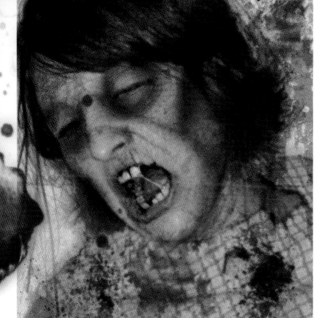

Louise Reeder
Captain

Jane Meyers

Steve Burke makes his point with a visiting team member during yet another undefeated season for the debate club.

Students from all walks of life make up the colorful mosaic that is the Racial Harmony Club!

AND we demand fresh intestines in the cafeteria!

Club President Joseph Cahill makes an impassioned plea for equality—the arc of justice is long but the arm of justice is ready to eat!

Clubs & Organizations
Future Insurance Salesmen of America

Todd Buell looks right at home behind a desk.

Just sign on the dotted line

Maryanne Andres, Carla Notz, and Jeannie Courtney plan for a fulfilling career in the insurance business—
uh, not life insurance, we hope!

Home Ec Club

Stephanie Olsen and Rhonda Franko iron out the wrinkles.

Marilyn Emery, Lorraine Prezell, and Judith Wade learn the ins and outs of seamstressry.

Someone's in the kitchen with Dina

Kathy Elia, Shirley McKassen, and Sandra Barda whip up something unusual in the kitchen. We like ours rare, girls!

Clubs & Organizations
Science Project Club

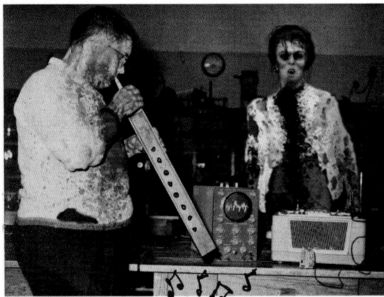

Studying the effects of an electrical current —careful, everyone!

Donald Baxter presents the most delicious portions of the human brain (the one you've got in your mouth!)

Where's my legs?

Dinner?

Yvette has "Crabs"

Yvette Cizek and Kenny Neary dismember a crayfish. Practice makes perfect.

"COME IN RANGOON"

The boys from the Short-Wave Radio club gather to hear News of the World—when will zombies walk on the moon? And what will they eat, when they do?!

The Projector Club's Bi-Weekly Friday Evening Movie Nights were quite the crowd-pleaser.

This talented group of thespians provided our school with many hours of charming shows and delightful shenanigans—legs were definitely broken.

Hey, Gwen Verdon?

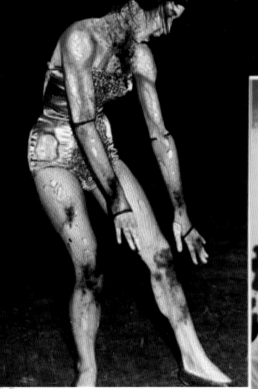

whatever Lola wants...

Ben Franklin?
Voltaire?
Dante?.
Doris Day??

How do you call a baritone sax player? Euphonium? (handwritten)

Constance Brown
Flute

James Burkheard
Saxophone & Trombone

Mary Elizabeth Hajny
Xylophone

Neil Olson
Keyboards

David Boehlke
Trumpet

Candy Ploshay
Clarinet & Oboe

Edwina Esposito
French Horn

Richard Polydoris
Director

♪ the thigh bone's connected ♪ to the thigh bone~ (handwritten)

My, that's a Big Baton! (handwritten)

Drum Major & Majorettes   Diane Hartanov; Pauline Harbour; Troy Jacobs; Edna Miles; AnnaLee Mohr

Student Gallery

From our printmaking class

Good job, Picasso!

A hilarious clown!

Sculpting from life

Lovely self-portrait

SOLD

Student Gallery

Tribute to a beloved pet

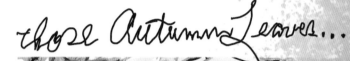

Spring is in the Air!

Sisters sit for a pastel portrait

Senior Autographs

Remember the fun we had in biology 101? Marcia Drake.

Make No bones about it. The future looks bright!! — Promises to keep

See you this Summer

Me! Lisa Flint '64

School Daze

PAIN

sunny

Becky Flint '64

Feed the hunger

Good Luck in Viet Nam

Best Wishes in all your ventures Steve Ritter '64

Please Please Me

Z

The woods are lovely, dark and deep. But I have miles to go before I sleep. aaaaaaaa rrrrrrrrrrrrrggggghhhhh

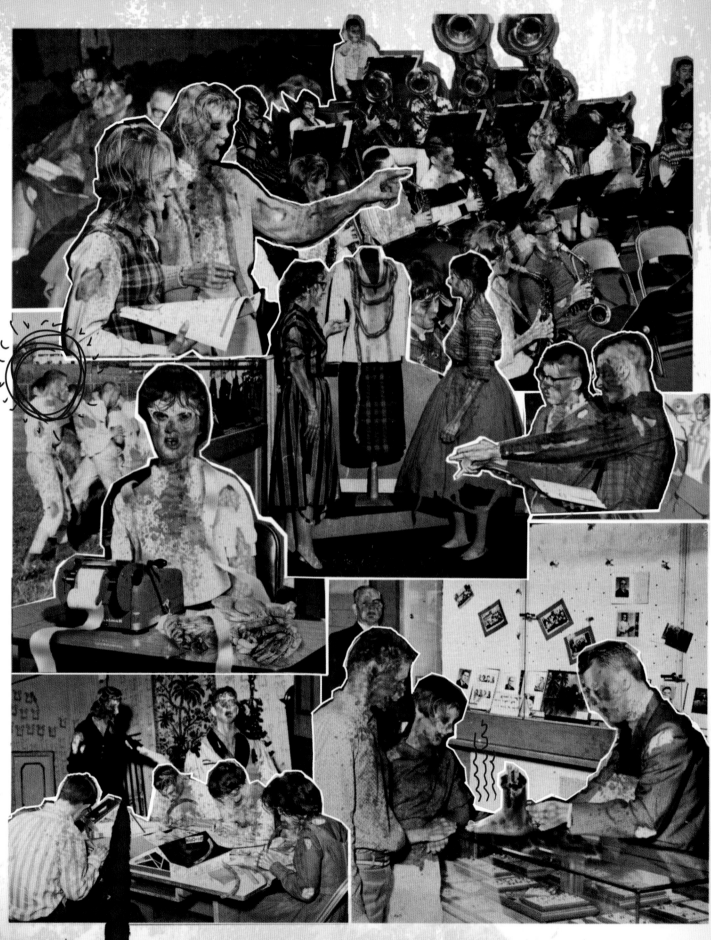

Regina Jordan, President; Gary Kelly, Vice President; Maurice Creel, Treasurer; Don Baskett, Secretary; Terry Camino, Sgt.-at-Arms; Dennis Silvey, Reporter; Barbra Robb, Inter-Club; Anita Gibson, Historian; Mary Phillips, Parliamentarian

Valedictorian
Ronald Graves

Alice '64
Newberry

Salutatorian
Alice Newberry

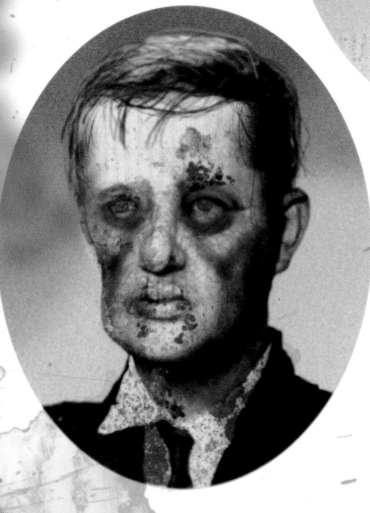

Good Citizenship
Judi Chiles

Good Citizenship Two - Shoes!

But ONLY
OneFoot

Good Citizenship
Milton Spencer

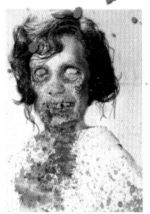
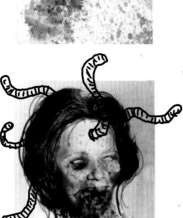

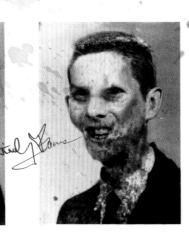

Aaron, Donna
"Thin is her hair, toothless her smile, her sweet personality makes friends all the while"
Language Club 2,3,4; Honor Society 3,4

Albert, Elaine
"She laughs from morning until night"
Pep Squad 2,3; Home Ec Club 1,2,3

Anderson, Peggy
"A girl of nimble wit is she, full of flies and gaiety"
Racial Harmony Club 3,4; Quill & Scroll 1,2,3

Armstrong, Dennis
"Don't take life too seriously, you'll never get out alive. Ever."
Football 1,2,3,4; Baseball 2,3; Debate Club 2,3

Bahr, Denise
"Call me"
Mathletes 1,2,3; Honor society 1,2,3,4

Barber, Bethany
"Where are my intestines?"
Homecoming Committee 3,4

Barnes, Christina
"There's no "I" in "MAGGOTS"
Glee 1,2

Brown, Rich
"Nothing was ever accomplished without enthusiasm"
Theater 2,3; Young Republicans 3; Languages 2,3,4; Basketball 3,4

Burbick, Grace
"The pain...the pain..."
Theater 1,2; Home Ec 2,3; Languages Club 1,2,4

Campbell, Sherry
"(unintelligible)"
Hall Monitor 2,3,4

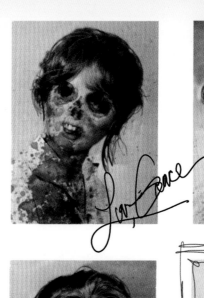
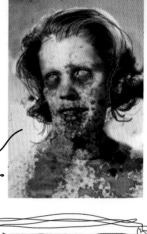

Crawford, Virginia
"Plenty of fish in the sea."
Pep Squad 1

Davies, Scott
"Every time you speak, your mind is on parade."
Science Project Club 1,2,3,4; Chess Club 3

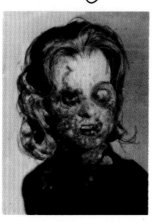

Davis, Thomas
"I love eye-juices."
Baseball 2,3; Basketball 1,2; Track 2,3

Dowd, Patricia
"Live and let live. More or less."
Home Ec Club 2,3,4; Sadie Hawkins Dance Committee
3,4; Girl's Field Hockey 2,3

Dyke, John
"Eat, drink and be merry."
Debate Club 2,3,4; Yearbook Staff 3,4; Honor Society 1,2

Edwards, Kirby
"Large in stature but gentle in nature."
Gymnastics 2,3

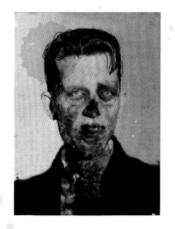
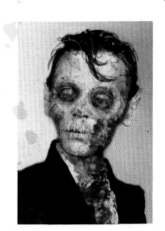

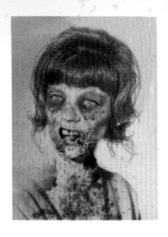
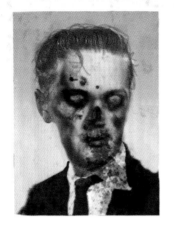

Fanning, Beatrice
"Studious."
Yearbook Staff 1,2,3,4; Home Ec Club 1,2,3,4; Racial Harmony Club 3,4

Feany, Bruce
"The hurrier I goes, the behinder I gets!"
Baseball 1,2; Football 2,3

Fincher, Sadie
"Not too serious, always gay, a fine friend in every way."
Rembrandt's Studio 2,3,4; Theater Club 1,2,3,4; Glee Club 3,4

Fischer, Marcella
"Carpet matches what's left of the drapes."
Hall Monitor 1

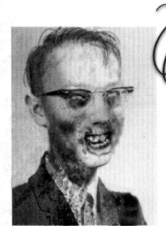

Fullerton, Carl
"Although quite studious, always fun and gay."
Baseball 1,2,3; Football 2,3; Cremation Detail 1,2,3,4

Gantz, Fred
"It isn't so much as the doing of things as the satisfaction of having it done."
Racial Harmony Club 3,4

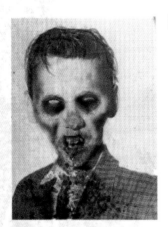

Gentile, John
"Why all this work and worry?"
Chess Club 1,2

Gerner, Marcia
"I ate my mailman this morning."
Honor Society 1,2,3,4

Hainey, Cherie
"Beware – I may yet do something memorable."
Languages Club 1,2; Prom Committee 3,4; Samhain
Committee 2,3,4

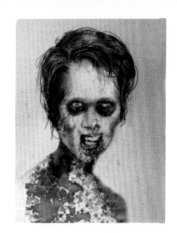
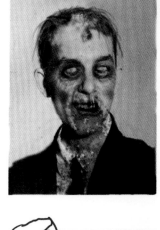

Harrold, Ronald
"Long pig"
Baseball 2,3; Basketball 1,2; Hall Monitor 3,4

...augh
...me Ec 1,2,3; Pep Squad 1

Hooper, Jerry
"Never do today what you can do tomorrow."
Racial Harmony Club 2,3; Languages Club 1,2,3,4; Honor
Society 1,2,3,4

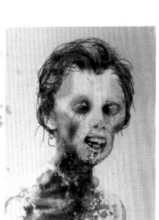
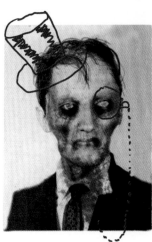

Hughes, Wanda
*"Wanda with her lovely hair, has a charm that's sweet and
rare."*
Young Republicans 2,3; Future Insurance Salesmen of
America 2,3

Jackson, Kenneth
"As many friends as those that know him?"
Blood & Organ Drive 3; Cafeteria Helper 1,2,3,4;
Cremation Detail 2,3,4

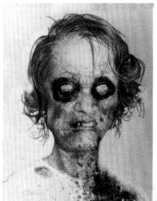
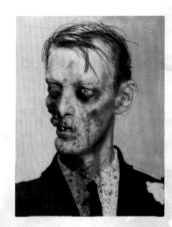

Jensen, Ruth
"I have worms in my nose."
Quill & Scroll Club 1,2; Glee Club 1,2,3,4

Johnson, Sharon
"She will succeed for she believes all she says."
Theater 1,2,3,4; Rembrandt's Studio 1,2,3,4

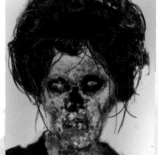
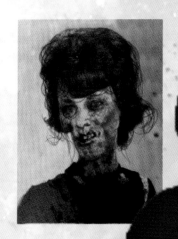

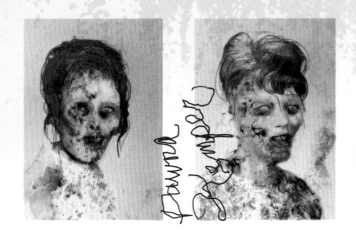

Karel, Catherine
"The future is ours."
Girl's Athletics 2,3; Honor society 1,2,3,4

Kemper, Dawna
"Studies are the least of my worries."
Homecoming Committee 1,2,3,4; Prom Committee 1,2,3,4;
Sadie Hawkins Committee 1,2,3,4; Samhain Committee
1,2,3,4; Glee Club 1,2,3,4; Racial Harmony Club 1,2,3,4

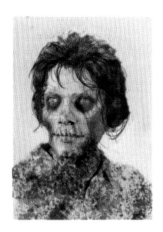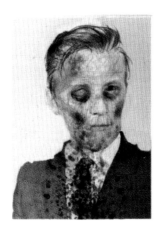

Kostner, Bonnie
*"Three things I'll miss about school: June, July and
BRRRAAAAAAAIIIINNNNNSSSSSSS."*
Crossing Guard 1

Kroll, Evan
*"No matter what is said or done, when Evan's around it's
always fun."*
Projector Club Assistant 1,2,3,4

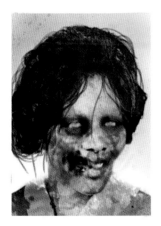

Laster, Rosalie
"Tramp"
Home Ec 1; Theater Club 1; Cafeteria Helper 2,3,4

Lease, Kay
"Quiet and innocent-looking but so is dynamite!"
Girls Athletics 1,2

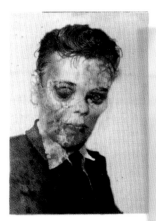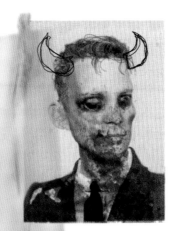

Lighter, Verne
"He who invented work should have finished it."
Rembrandt's Studio 2,3,4; Quill & Scroll 1,2; Cremation
Detail 3,4

Lyson, Stephen
"Punctual"
Glee Club 1,2,3,4

Mason, Jason
"There are two sides to every story – mine and the tasty, dripping one's."
Football 1,2,3; Gymnastics 2; Baseball 2,3; Yearbook Committee 3,4

Marsten, Robert
"What should a man do but be merry? Trip and fall, perhaps."
Science Project Club 3,4; Hall Monitor 2,3,4

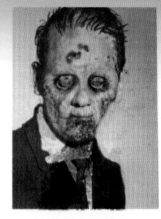

Meecham, Norma
"Life is short. Really short."
Theater Club 1,2,3,4; Glee Club 2,3

Meeks, Barry
"Make the pain go away…"
Cafeteria Helper 1,2,3,4; Home Ec 2,3,4; Baseball 1

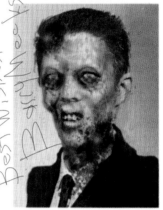

Miller, Grace
"Music is one of my many loves. Music and spleens."
Honor Society 2,3,4

Miller, Joanne
"Good things come in small packages."
Racial Harmony Club 2,3; Band Club 1,2,3,4

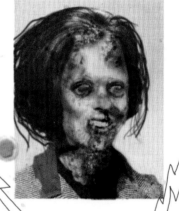
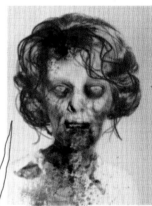

Morgan, Michael
"A penny saved is a penny something, something…"
Basketball 2,3; Baseball 1,2,3; Young Republicans 1,2

Nagel, Ray
"Better a diamond with a flaw than a pebble without."
Chess Club 1,2,3,4; Debate Club 1,2; Short Wave Radio Club 2,3; Hall Monitor 1,2,3,4; Crossing Guard 1,2,3,4

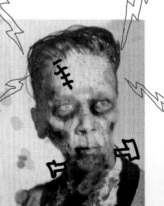

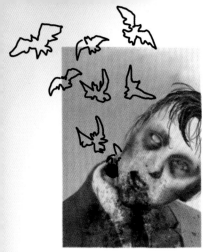

Nestor, Ralph
"Remember the Golden Rule: Eat Lest Ye Be Eaten."
Football 2; Baseball 2,3

Nixon, Curt
"Are you going to eat this?"
Yearbook Committee 2,3,4; Quill & Scroll Club 1,2,3,4

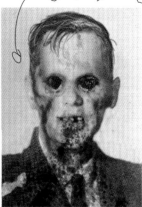

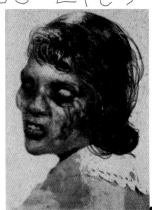

Noonan, Thomas
"He who speaks without modesty will find it difficult to make his words good."
Gymnastics 2,3; Racial Harmony Club 1,2

North, Regina
"Braaaaaiiiiinnnnnnnnnssssssssss…"
Honor Society 3,4; Yearbook Committee 2,3,4; Mathlete 2,3

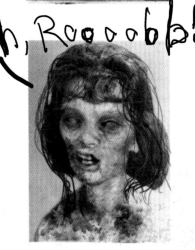

Nutterman, Craig
"A man may die, nations may rise and fall, but an idea lives on."
Football 2,3; Baseball 1,2

Oaks, Bernice
"Three can keep a secret, if two of them are undead."
Homecoming Committee 2,3,4; Prom Committee 2,3,4; Glee Club 1,2

Oatley, Susanna
"Where's my foot?"
Chess Club 1,2,3,4

Otis, Francesca
"A house divided against itself cannot stand."
Home Ec 2,3,4; Cafeteria Helper 3,4; Theater Club 1,2,3,4

Passy, Donald
"Tact is the ability to describe others as they see them-selves."
Hall Monitor 3,4; Debate Club 3,4

Patrick, Davis
"Something is oozing."
Science Project Club 2,3,4; Yearbook Committee 3,4; Quill
& Scroll 2,3; Band Club 2; Honor Society 2

Paul, Ronald
"A coward is much more exposed to quarrels than a man of spirit."
Future Insurance Salesmen of America 1,2,3,4; Short
Wave Radio Club 2,3

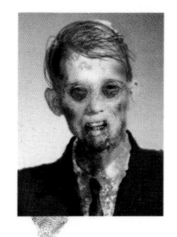

Peterson, Sandy
"There is nothing like fun, is there?"
Hall Monitor 1,2,3,4; Academic Decathlon 1,2,3

Piper, Mary
"Make it a double."
Racial Harmony Club 1; Debate Club 3,4; Honor Society
3,4

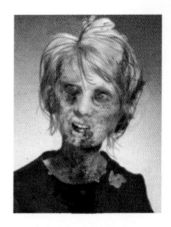

Platter, Yvonne
"Go Cubbies!"

Quackenbush, Steven
"He who loves not brains, viscera, and song remains a fool his whole life long."
Basketball 2; Baseball 1,2,3; Gymnastics 1

Quail, Amy
"Few men have virtue to withstand the highest bidder."
Girl's Athletics 1,2,3; Pep Squad 2,3; Prom Committee 3,4;
Sadie Hawkins Dance 1,2,3,4; Theater 2,3

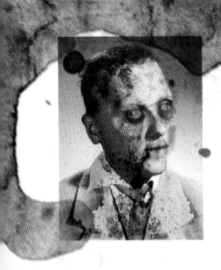

Quincy, George
"Ouch!"
Basketball 1; Baseball 2,3

"eh, sonny?"

Rancick, Leo
"A pint of sweat saves a gallon of blood."
Cremation Detail 1,2,3,4

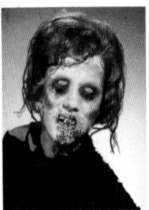
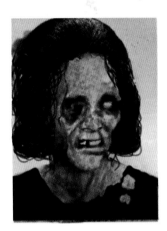

Redman, Shirley
"Don't let the fear of striking out hold you back."
Glee Club 1,2,3,4; Theater 1,2,3,4

Reed, Violet
"Equality for all!"
Racial Harmony Club 3,4; Home Ec 2,3,4

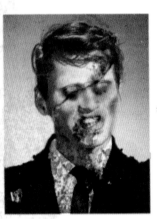
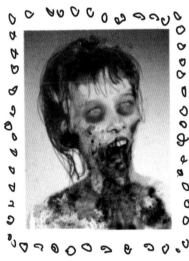

Reese, Stanley
"Life is a dream."
Football 2,3,4

Richmond, Darlene
"An admirable wit, and always the friendliest."
Homecoming Committee 2,3,4; Samhain Committee 3,4

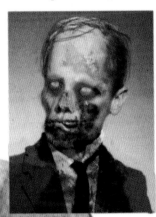

Richter, Allen
"A real nice guy."
Baseball 1,2,3; Gymnastics 1; Mathletes 2,3; Academic Decathlon 1,2

Rose, Gary
"The only way to have a friend is to be one."
Band Club 1,2,3,4

Russo, Raymond
"Big Ray – a sense of humor and a loyal friend."
Honor Society 3,4; Hall Monitor 1,2,3

Salvio, Carol Anne
"Her eye shines only for one."
Languages Club 2,3,4; Rembrandt's Studio 2,3,4

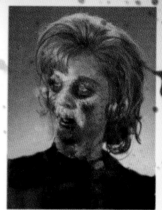

Schaeffer, June
"Tiny and petite – but oh so fond of meat."
Glee Club 1,2,3; Theater Club 2,3,4; Girls Athletics 2,3

Severini, Maria
"No-Legs"
Cafeteria Helper 2,3,4

Shimko, Peggy
"Determination plus"
Pep Squad 1,2; Homecoming Committee 2,3,4; Prom Committee 1,2,3,4

Smith, Rodney
"You might see Rodney around the Pole, for Seward's icebox is his goal."
Basketball 1,2; Cremation Detail 2,3,4

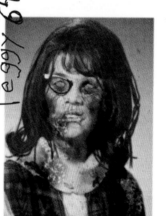
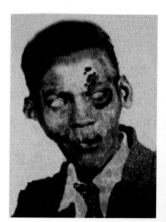

Best Wishes, Peggy '64

Smith, Terry
"Pleasant"
Debate Club 3,4; Honor Society 2,3,4

Sweitzer, Margaret
"It took a tiger to tame her – look at the gleam in her eye!"
Girls Athletics 1,3; Glee Club 2,3,4

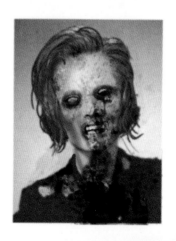

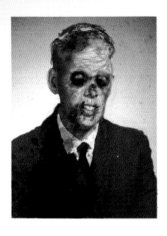

Sweston, Todd
Did not graduate

Tanner, Elwood
"A friend to all with a heart of gold"
Languages Club 2; Mathlete 2,3

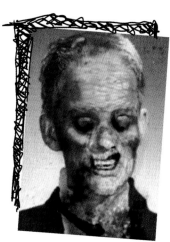

Tenston, Jerry
"Another nice guy."
Gymnastics 1,2; Young Republicans 1,2; Academic
Decathlon 2; Honor Society 2,3,4

Tinsdale, Ronald
"His exotic interests will lead him to many lands."
Cafeteria Helper 1,2,3,4; Projector Club 1,2

Edwina Ulster

Ulster, Edwina
"A gingerbread princess of sugar and spice. And pus."
Racial Harmony Club 2,3; Rembrandt's Studio 1,2,3; Year-
book Committee 3,4

Urlacher, Orville
"Quite a beau!"
Chess Club 2,3,4; Hall Monitor 1

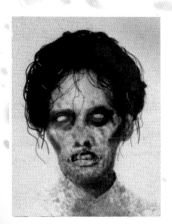

Utton, Paulette
"Sweet, Petite, and a treat to meet."
Glee Club 1,2,4; Pep Squad 2,3; Prom Committee 2,3,4

Van Kamp, Lisa
"She gives her love to all, but her heart to only one."
Home Ec 1,3; Blood & Organ Drive 3

Vetter, Randall
"Uh-Oh"

Via, Gary
"Neato"
Baseball 2,3; Basketball 1,2,3; Debate Club 3,4

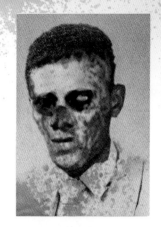

Voigt, Vaughan
"There are three things on his mind – cars, girls, and brains."
Quill & Scroll 1; Short Wave Radio Club 1,2,3; Honor Society 2,3,4

Watkins, Penelope
"A merry heart maketh a cheerful countenance."
Cafeteria Helper 3,4; Hall Monitor 1,2,3; Racial Harmony Club 1

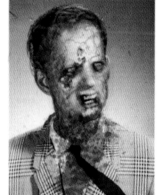

Warnick, Marshall
"A major leaguer in any league."
Football 2,3; Baseball 3

Williams, John
"I like math."
Mathlete 1,2; Academic Decathlon 2,3; Honor Society 2,3,4; Projector Club 1,2; Science Project Club 2,3,4

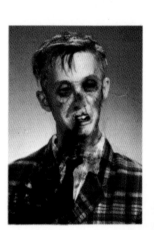

Zislo, Gail
"Pretty good at sports – for a girl!"
Girl's Athletics 2,3; Pep Squad 1,2,3; Band Club 3

Zuflo, Crawford
"Do unto others before they do unto you."
Home Ec 2,3,4; Samhain Committee 2,3,4; Prom Committee 3,4; Yearbook Committee 2,3,4

Junior Autographs

Call me this Summer! Debbie Beyer

Stay in touch!

See you this Summer ~Dave

'89

You've got me under your skin!

Go reformed Druids of North America

the "Mop Tops"

please make the pain stop —Susie V.

The worms crawl in, the worms crawl out...

Please stay in touch

Z

A GORE-US Line!

Junior Class Officers

David Freeman, President; Anita Bowman, Treasurer; Helen Myers, Secretary; Skip Wenner, Vice President; Mary Hewitt, Reporter; Steve Timmons, Sgt.-at-Arms; JoeLytle, Historian

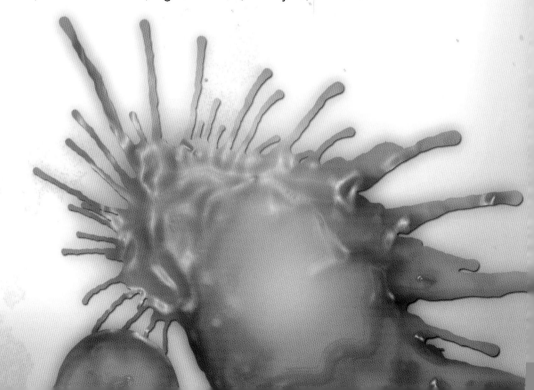

Junior Blood & Organ Drive

Blood type?
"B" positive!

JoEllen Myers

Jerome Bookwalter

Adams, Steve
Alder, Robert
Allen, Mary
Anderson, Donald

offerings to Cthulu!

Austin, Mike
Baker, Delores
Barnes, Eva
Bender, Thomas

Shrieking in the darkness

Bowman, William
Calloway, Cynthia
Cassidy, John
Clark, Linda

at the Mountains of Madness

DeWitt, James
Dougherty, Jim
East, Connie
Eller, Vince

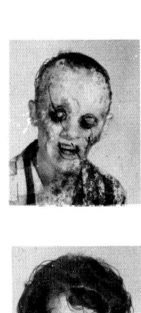
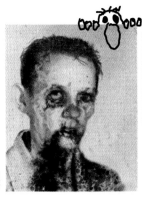
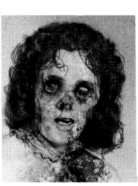
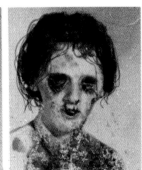

Estes, Stephen

Farrell, Carl

Fischer, Ruth

Fitzgerald, Elaine

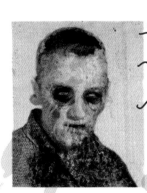
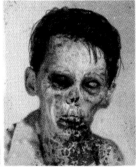
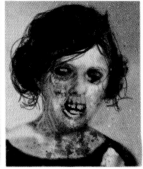
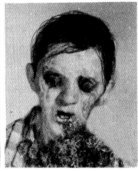

Fretzer, Jill

Gaines, Robbie

Gallagher, Pat

Galloway, Bill

Mary

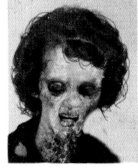
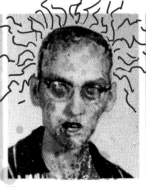
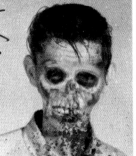
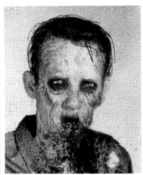

Garr, Tim

Grimm, Thom

Hahn, Bill

Hamilton, Joe

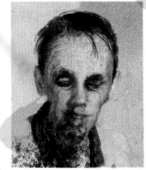
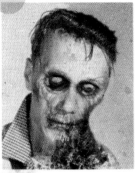
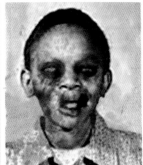
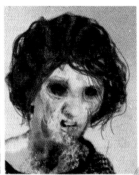

Harrison, Larry

Henson, Michael

Hoover, Jerry

Jackson, Darlene

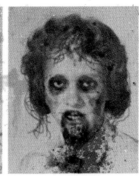
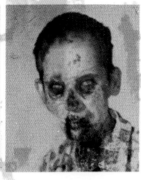
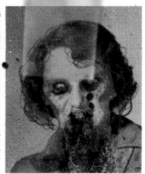

Jameson, Sue Ellen
Johnson, Bob
Jones, Karen
Justice, Alice

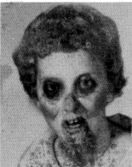
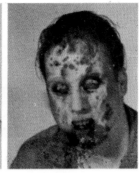
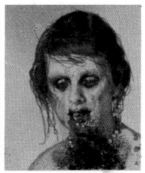

Kaye, Beth
Keene, Nancy
Keller, Robert
Koeppen, Marie

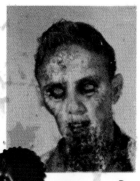
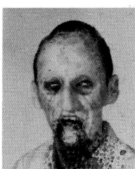
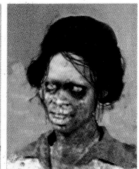
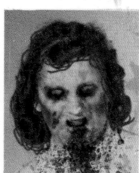

Koons, Teddy
Lang, Wilbur
Lansford, LaVerne
Larson, Patrice

♫ Go Away, Little Ghoul

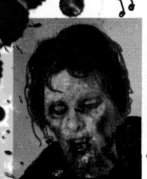
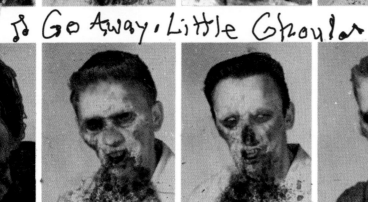
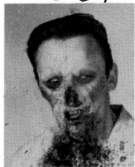

Lawson, Judy
Little, Irvin
McKee, Dwayne
Macy, Davie

Martin, Claire

Meyer, Rhonda

Miller, Earl

Nagel, Evelyn

Newsom, Bruce

Newton, Lynette

Noonan, Martin

Oakley, Lawrence

Otis, Geoffrey

Otts, Willa

Owen, Fred

Palmer, James

Packer, Ro

Peterson,

Price, Mort

Ray, Anita

It's my Party~Leslie GORE!

Ha Ha Ha Ha ha ha ha haaaaaassss

the 9Hell?

Reed, Mary Ellen
Reid, Heather
Samuel, Mike
Skelton, Harvey

Smith, Eugene
Smith, Joann
Staggs, Leroy
Stuart, Patrick

Studebacker, Sue
Thomas, David
Thomas, Kathaleen
Tiller, Ellen

Tucker, Connie
Underwood, Harvey
Upton, Dean
Usher, Roger

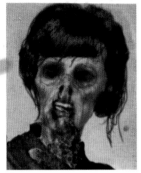
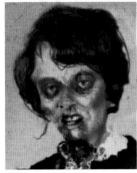
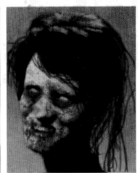

Vance, Betty

Wallace, Marcella

Walter, Judith

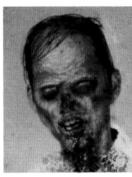

Ward, Mona

Warner, Charles

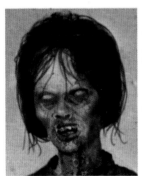
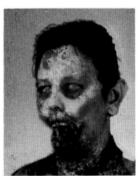
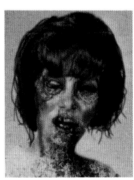

Williams, Shirley

Willis, James

Young, Helen

Junior Prom Committee
Members spend a little time
outside after a snack

It was fun sitting next to the BRAINIEST kid in school! Delicious! Never forget Mrs. Sumner's sweetbreads in Home Ec!

See you this Summer... lots of free time to FEED!

Dismember me!

2 GOOD
+ 2 BE
= 4 DINNER

Welcome!

Scream the long moan with the Jeannie entrails...

Welcome, Sylvia Plath Z

Sophomore Class Officers

Dave Perry, President; Anna Quigly, Treasurer; Steve Wilkes, Vice President;
Bruce Davies, Historian; Mary Ellen Smith, Reporter; Irving Bell, Sgt.-at-Arms

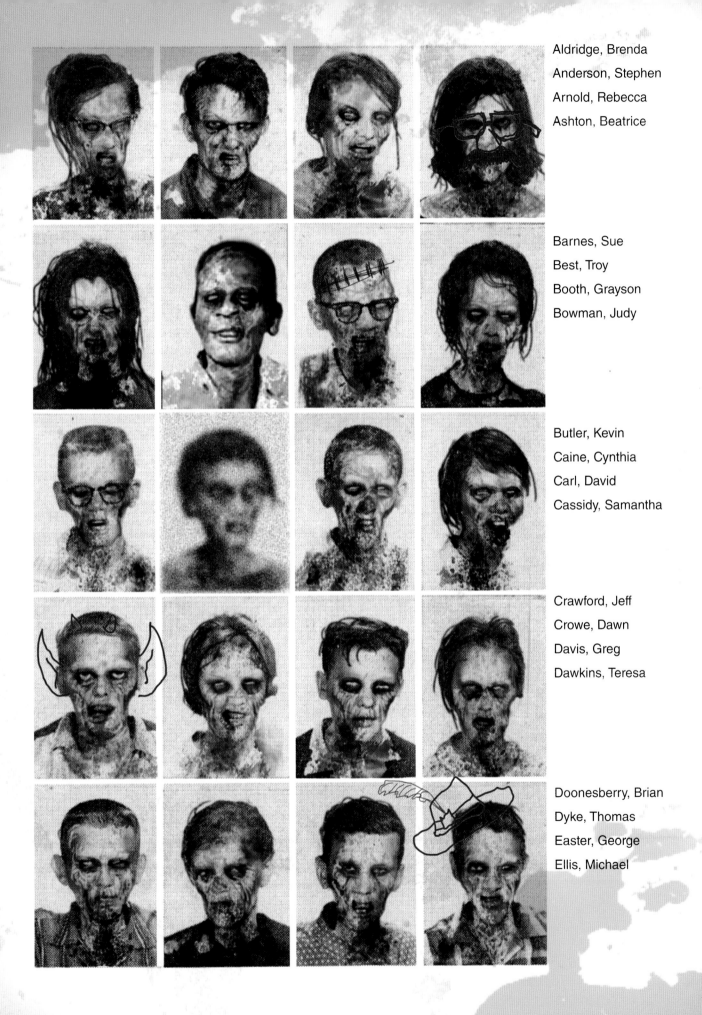

Aldridge, Brenda

Anderson, Stephen

Arnold, Rebecca

Ashton, Beatrice

Barnes, Sue

Best, Troy

Booth, Grayson

Bowman, Judy

Butler, Kevin

Caine, Cynthia

Carl, David

Cassidy, Samantha

Crawford, Jeff

Crowe, Dawn

Davis, Greg

Dawkins, Teresa

Doonesberry, Brian

Dyke, Thomas

Easter, George

Ellis, Michael

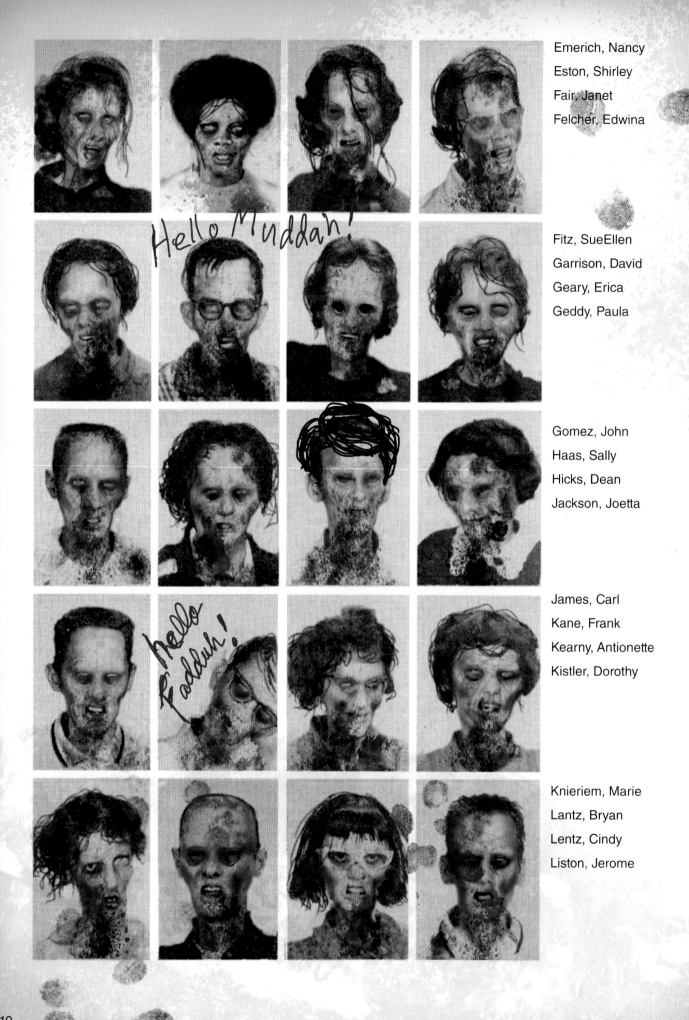

Emerich, Nancy
Eston, Shirley
Fair, Janet
Felcher, Edwina

Fitz, SueEllen
Garrison, David
Geary, Erica
Geddy, Paula

Gomez, John
Haas, Sally
Hicks, Dean
Jackson, Joetta

James, Carl
Kane, Frank
Kearny, Antionette
Kistler, Dorothy

Knieriem, Marie
Lantz, Bryan
Lentz, Cindy
Liston, Jerome

110

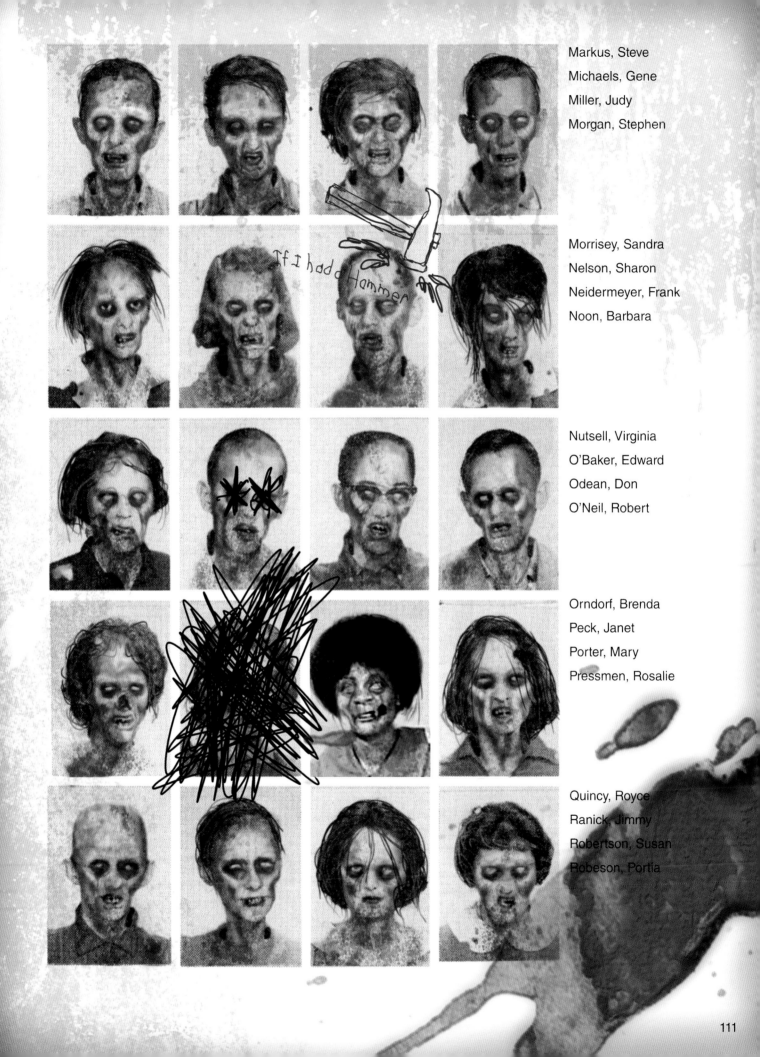

Markus, Steve
Michaels, Gene
Miller, Judy
Morgan, Stephen

Morrisey, Sandra
Nelson, Sharon
Neidermeyer, Frank
Noon, Barbara

Nutsell, Virginia
O'Baker, Edward
Odean, Don
O'Neil, Robert

Orndorf, Brenda
Peck, Janet
Porter, Mary
Pressmen, Rosalie

Quincy, Royce
Ranick, Jimmy
Robertson, Susan
Robeson, Portia

111

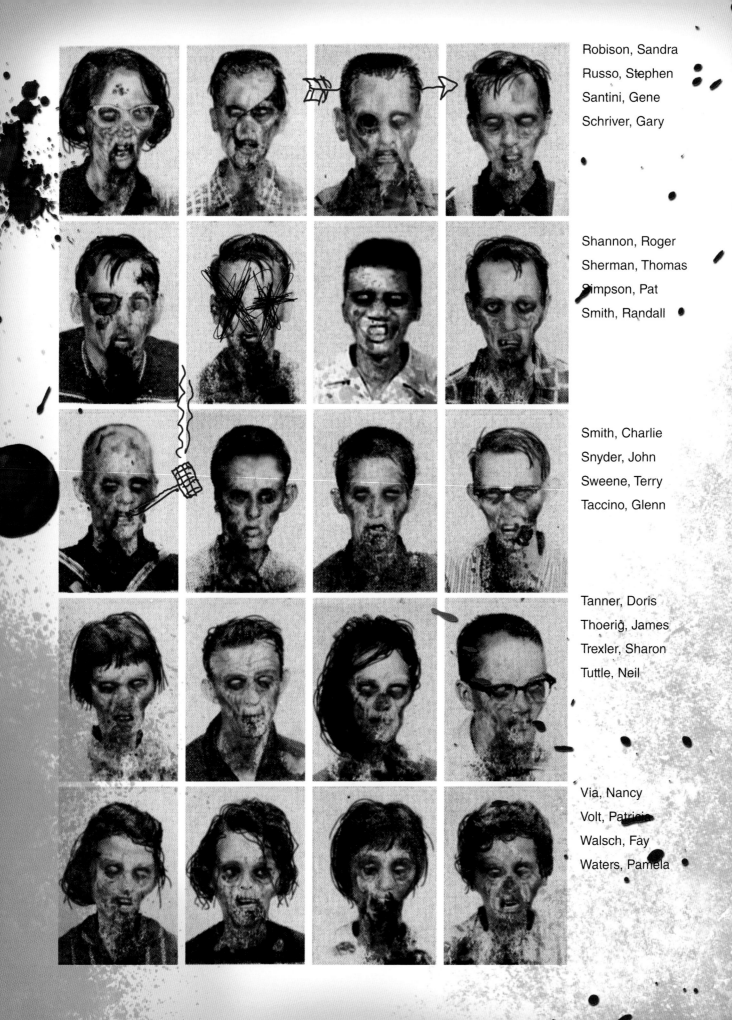

Robison, Sandra
Russo, Stephen
Santini, Gene
Schriver, Gary

Shannon, Roger
Sherman, Thomas
Simpson, Pat
Smith, Randall

Smith, Charlie
Snyder, John
Sweene, Terry
Taccino, Glenn

Tanner, Doris
Thoerig, James
Trexler, Sharon
Tuttle, Neil

Via, Nancy
Volt, Patricia
Walsch, Fay
Waters, Pamela

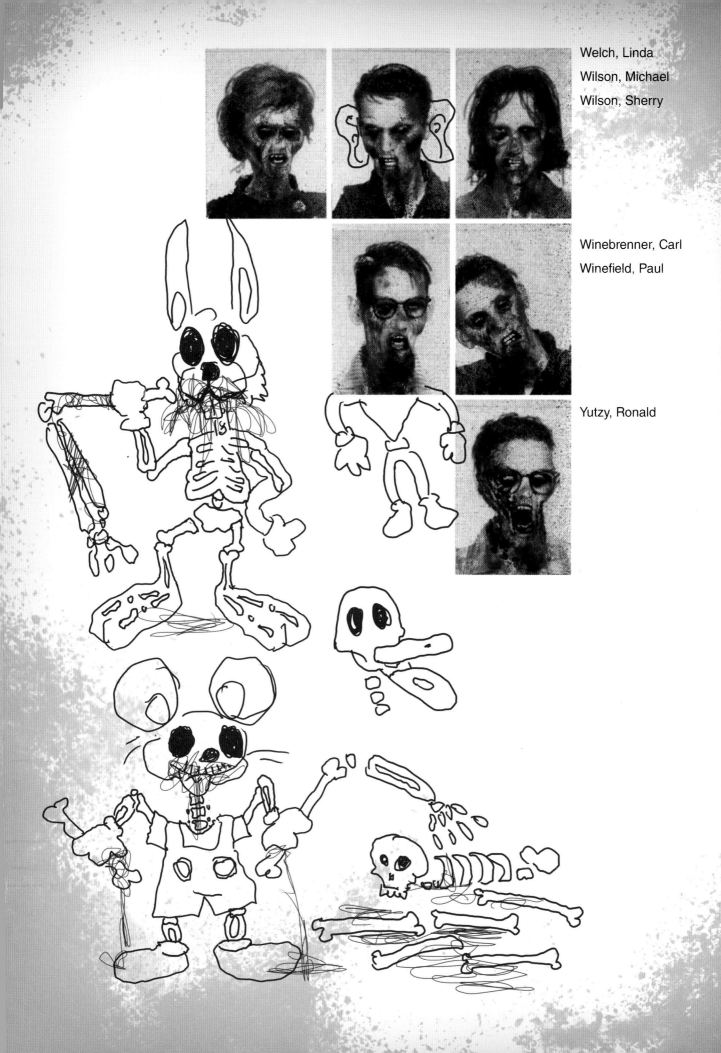

Welch, Linda

Wilson, Michael

Wilson, Sherry

Winebrenner, Carl

Winefield, Paul

Yutzy, Ronald

On this page of pearly white it looked so good i took a BITE...

ii lots ii

make

"Walk like a man, talk like a mom" unless you have no vocal cords or legs!

There are 3 sides to any argument— your side, my side, and the right side (of the brain)

marry a girl for her BRAINS

sweet yummy Brains

Keep your smile intact
Connie Schoff '04

BrainSSSSSSSSSSS

Z

Freshman Memories

DUCK AND COVER!

Freshman Class Officers

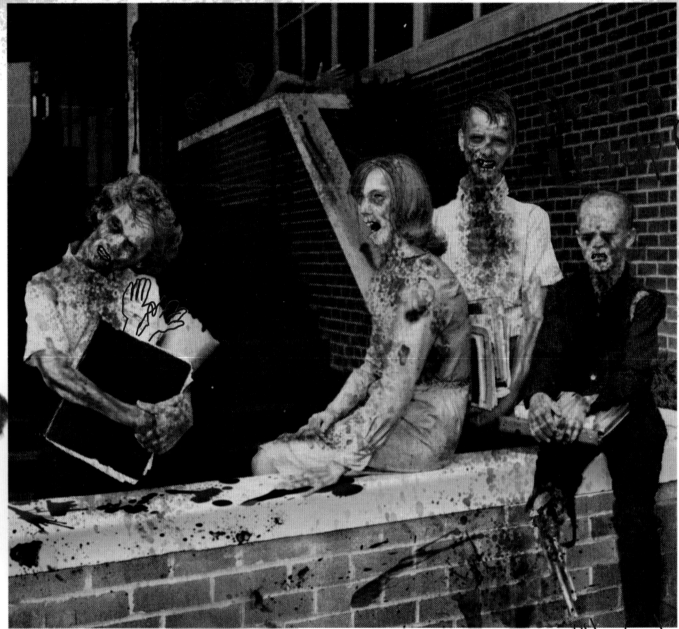

Pauline Snyder, President; Victoria Rankin, Treasurer; Stephen Garlock, Vice President; Kenny "Stumps" Higgins, Reporter

Freshman Bake Sale

She's no Donna Reed

M,m,M,m,M,m,3!

Spleen Cakes .10

Tendon Treats .10

Gall Balls .15

Appendix Nuggets .15

Nose Scraps

es of "68"
ke Sale

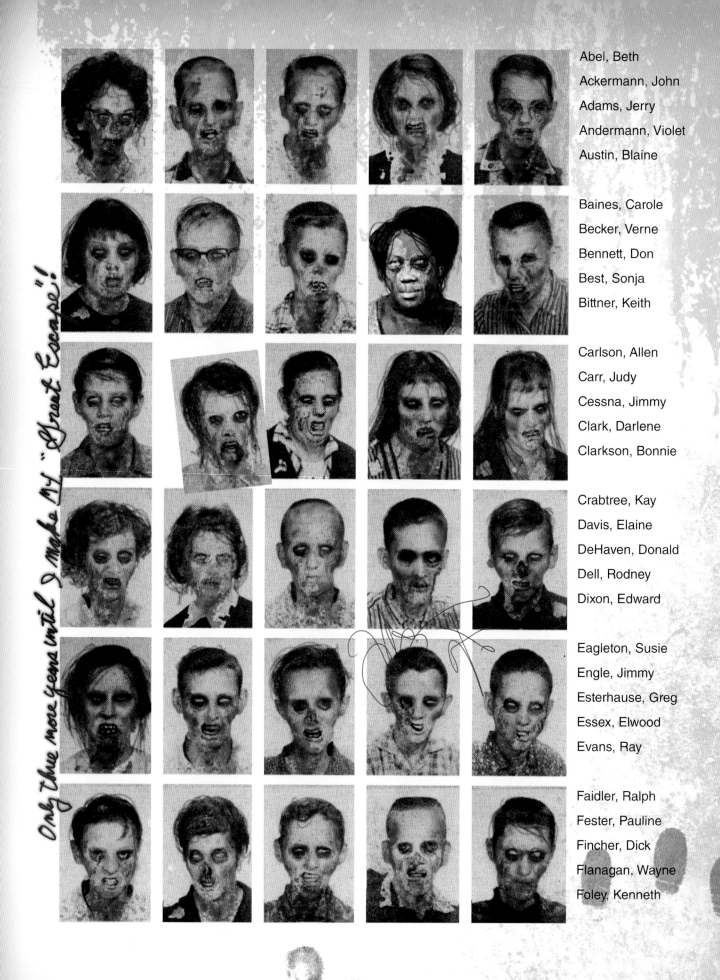

Abel, Beth
Ackermann, John
Adams, Jerry
Andermann, Violet
Austin, Blaine

Baines, Carole
Becker, Verne
Bennett, Don
Best, Sonja
Bittner, Keith

Carlson, Allen
Carr, Judy
Cessna, Jimmy
Clark, Darlene
Clarkson, Bonnie

Crabtree, Kay
Davis, Elaine
DeHaven, Donald
Dell, Rodney
Dixon, Edward

Eagleton, Susie
Engle, Jimmy
Esterhause, Greg
Essex, Elwood
Evans, Ray

Faidler, Ralph
Fester, Pauline
Fincher, Dick
Flanagan, Wayne
Foley, Kenneth

Only three more years until I make MY "Great Escape"!

118

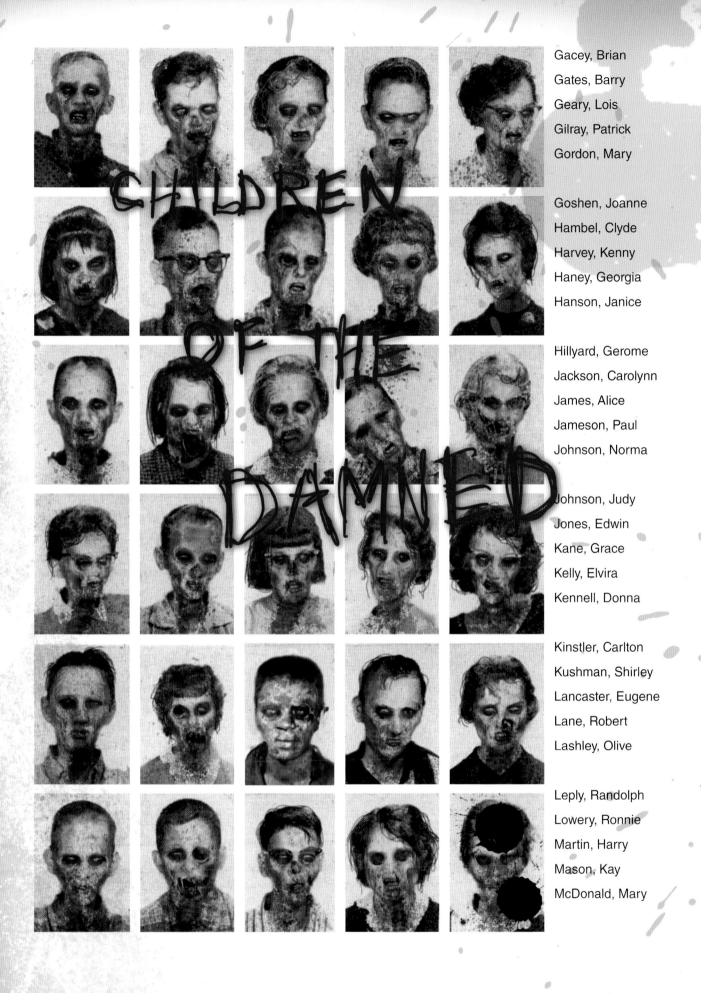

CHILDREN OF THE DAMNED

Gacey, Brian

Gates, Barry

Geary, Lois

Gilray, Patrick

Gordon, Mary

Goshen, Joanne

Hambel, Clyde

Harvey, Kenny

Haney, Georgia

Hanson, Janice

Hillyard, Gerome

Jackson, Carolynn

James, Alice

Jameson, Paul

Johnson, Norma

Johnson, Judy

Jones, Edwin

Kane, Grace

Kelly, Elvira

Kennell, Donna

Kinstler, Carlton

Kushman, Shirley

Lancaster, Eugene

Lane, Robert

Lashley, Olive

Leply, Randolph

Lowery, Ronnie

Martin, Harry

Mason, Kay

McDonald, Mary

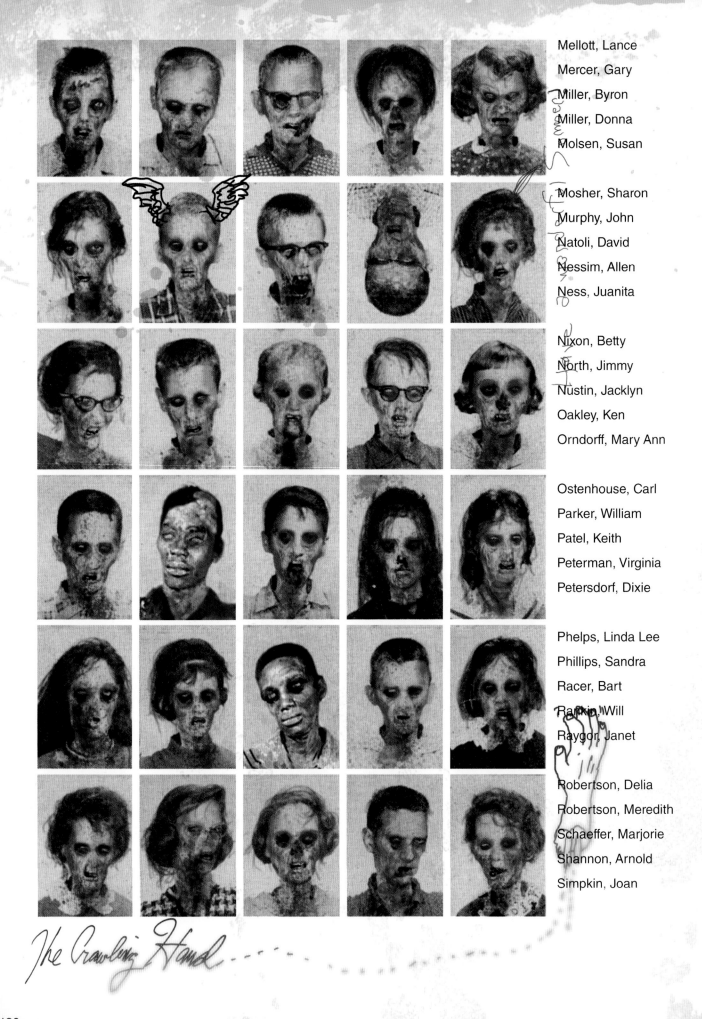

Mellott, Lance

Mercer, Gary

Miller, Byron

Miller, Donna

Molsen, Susan

Mosher, Sharon

Murphy, John

Natoli, David

Nessim, Allen

Ness, Juanita

Nixon, Betty

North, Jimmy

Nustin, Jacklyn

Oakley, Ken

Orndorff, Mary Ann

Ostenhouse, Carl

Parker, William

Patel, Keith

Peterman, Virginia

Petersdorf, Dixie

Phelps, Linda Lee

Phillips, Sandra

Racer, Bart

Rankin, Will

Raygor, Janet

Robertson, Delia

Robertson, Meredith

Schaeffer, Marjorie

Shannon, Arnold

Simpkin, Joan

The Crawling Hand

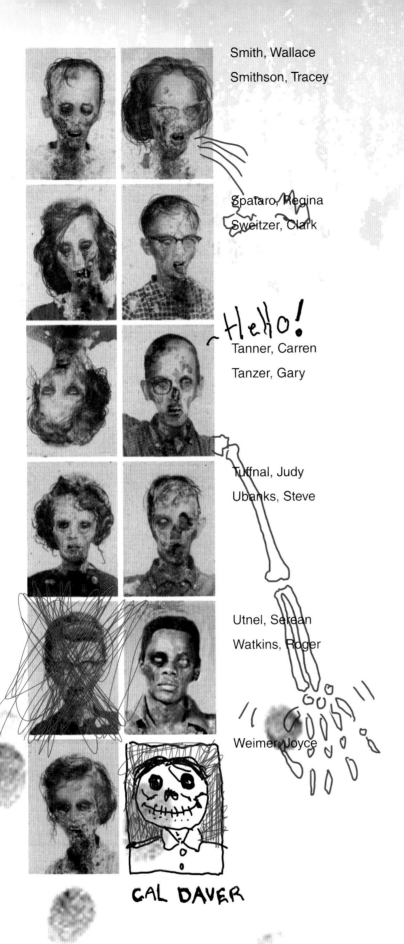

Smith, Wallace

Smithson, Tracey

Spataro, Regina

Sweitzer, Clark

~Hello!

Tanner, Carren

Tanzer, Gary

Tuffnal, Judy

Ubanks, Steve

Utnel, Serean

Watkins, Roger

Weimer, Joyce

CAL DAVER

In Memoriam

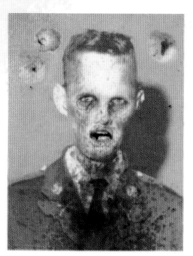

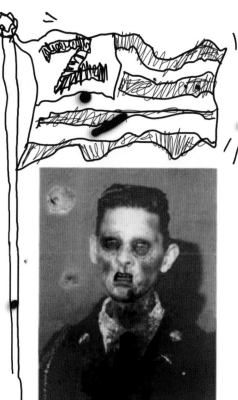

ROTC Members Bill Wilcox, David Spears, and Charlie Griffin all met untimely second deaths due to an unfortunate shooting range mishap.

In addition, Dean Guinn and Sol Fischer had to be put down after the incident due to the unusual nature of their injuries.

Former Theater Director Mr. Frapasella and five students were immolated in an unexplained electrical fire.

The west wing of the auditorium suffered substantial damage due to the fire.

In Memoriam

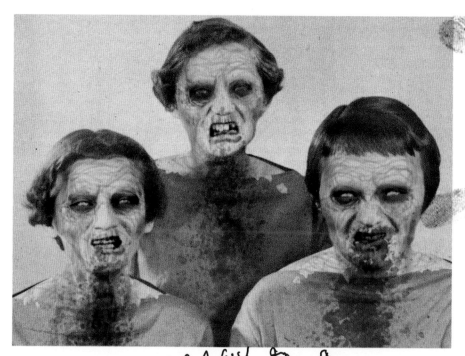

The talented Meakin Sisters were all three decapitated instantaneously when crossing Main Street in March. They always traveled hand in hand and sadly it was this charming habit that allowed them to be cut down so easily, like a row of lovely spring daffodils.

Our Sponsors

Burke's Fluids & Secretions

A quart a day...
keeps decomposition at bay!

15 South Post Street   Phone 4481

Be a Telephone Girl!

You'll be smart if you
look now into the possibilities of
a job as a Telephone Operator
after graduation.
See your Vocational Guidance
Counselor for more information
about these opportunities.

Monday through Friday
8:30 A.M. to 5:00 P.M.

STATE TELEPHONE COMPANY
42 W. 60th Street
Evans City

Planning Your Future? Why Bother?

Marriage? College? Are you really
looking to make any long-term plans after graduation?
If you are seriously considering this, then start saving
NOW for the Big Day. Odds are you won't get another chance.
Make regular deposits in a School Savings account at
Evans State Band. It's quick and easy. Just ask your
homeroom teacher for an E.S.B. Deposit Card, fill it out,
return it with your deposit and that's it! Save somthing EVERY
banding day.
You don't have much time left.

Evans Savings Bank

the corner of Oak and Main
Phone 3451

Grim's Evans Crest Beauty Salon

Restoration   Repair   Replacement

1313 Mockingbird Lane   Phone 4382

AAA Cleaners

Dirt? Grease? Blood? Bile?
Please see us for all your dry cleaning needs

213 Fourth Street   Phone 3232

L.L. Wendt Agency

Insurers – Realtors

Just in case you make it out of high school

19 Front Street   Phone 3822

125

Our Sponsors

for those us with ears!

Hear! Hear!

For the finest in music,
please consider

Meyer's Music Mart

328 North State Street

Join the People Who Know
Kresge's is the place to go.

Kresge's

19 W. Chestnut   Phone 3328

Join the "Swing" to Gas

Stop in and look over
our appliances, won't you?

West-Central Pennsylvania Public Service Company

422 Eleventh St.   Phone 3181

Karel's Greenhouse

Roses are red
Violets are blue
I'm quite dead
and so are you

Next to Werner's Funeral Home
on State Street
Phone 2886

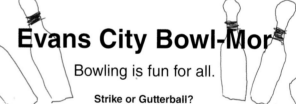

Evans City Bowl-Mor

Bowling is fun for all.

Strike or Gutterball?

Savini Printing & Lithography

These Changing Times
Do not affect the High-Quality Service
we provide

433 Fourth Street   Phone 3299

Get your Balls out of the Gutter!

Come down and see for yourself

72 E. Market   Phone 4256

Our Sponsors

General Tire and Rubber Manufacturing

For all your tire and rubber needs

566 Park   **Phone 7434**

Eva's Diner

for the "very best" pie in the county
Open 5:00 A.M. Every Day

7 E. Douglas Street
Extra Parking In Rear

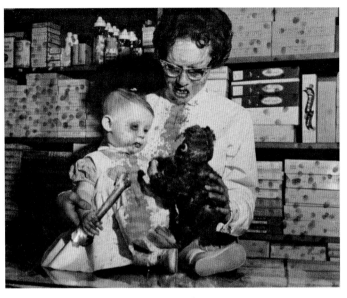

Lerner's Children Shop
Toddlers and Children
Through Fourteen

Clothing   **Blankets**   **Shoes**

Bed Linens   **Chew Toys**   **Muzzles**

923 Thirteenth Street   **Phone 3228**

For the unusual in gifts

The best candy you ever tasted,
holiday cards and wrappings,
fountain pens and stationery,
please visit

Spellington's Gift Shop

501 Erie   **Phone 6672**

Werner's Funeral Home and Crematorium

400 State Street

*Dignified Service For
All Your Post-Life Needs*

Phone 1345

Knock on Wood

Dick's
Furnance Repair

Will you be ready this Fall?

Ask For Big Dick!

And his cousin I. P. Frealy!

712 Market   **Phone 3462**

127

Our Sponsors

STERLING and the distinctive Sterling logo are registered trademarks of Sterling Publishing Co., Inc.

10 9 8 7 6 5 4 3 2 1

Published by Sterling Publishing Co., Inc.
387 Park Avenue South, New York, NY 10016
© 2011 by Jeff Busch
Distributed in Canada by Sterling Publishing
c/o Canadian Manda Group, 165 Dufferin Street
Toronto, Ontario, Canada M6K 3H6
Distributed in the United Kingdom by GMC Distribution Services
Castle Place, 166 High Street, Lewes,
East Sussex, England BN7 1XU
Distributed in Australia by Capricorn Link (Australia) Pty. Ltd.
P.O. Box 704, Windsor, NSW 2756, Australia

Printed in China

Sterling ISBN 978-1-4027-8471-2

For information about custom editions, special sales, premium and corporate purchases, please contact Sterling Special Sales Department at 800-805-5489 or specialsales@sterlingpublishing.com.

Sincere thanks to my editor Nathaniel Marunas, Emily Meithner and Jason Prince. Extra special thanks to the talented and all-knowing Dave Hoyt, gadabout cartoonist extraordinaire Bill King and, most importantly, my lovely and patient wife Michelle.

For all your Undead news and products, please visit www.zombie-universe.com and www.facebook.com/zombieuniverse